Lizzie Watts

Her life, her family and her war

PHIL WATTS

First published in the United Kingdom in 2021 by
The Cloister House Press

ISBN 978-1-913460-44-0

For Carol, who helped start me on the very slippery, but fascinating, slope of Family History.

For Andy and Karon, who helped persuade me that this was a story worth telling.

For my amazing wife and soulmate, Brigid, without whose insights, questions, suggestions and proof reading this book would have been so much the poorer although any errors remaining are strictly my own. Without her support, understanding and patience more time would have been spent tackling the 'To Do' lists and far less time researching and writing.

Lastly, of course, for Lizzie, without whom there would have been no tale to tell. I hope that she would recognise herself as the strong, resilient, loving woman, wife and mother that I have found her to be.

This is the biography of my great grandmother Lizzie Watts (born Elizabeth Hone, 1863-1933). I was motivated to try and capture her and her family's remarkable life and times from the research I have been carrying out on my family's heritage and ancestry. As I uncovered events and circumstances in the family history, more and more seemed to coalesce around the life and times of Lizzie Watts. The interest of friends, with whom I shared some of these, persuaded me that, perhaps, here was a story worth the telling, spanning the 60 years between the mid-Victorian period to just after the First World War.

The question arose of how to give my great grandmother a voice after all these years. I finally decided that it would take the form of a conversation with her grandson, Sydney, my father.

The facts and events in the book have been carefully researched and are also referenced to family memories, photographs and heirlooms handed down the generations. Some of the detail of the dialogue has been imagined for the purpose of continuity and to bring her story to life. However some details are also courtesy of the prodigious memory of my father, who could recount conversations almost verbatim decades after they happened, and who shared many of these with me over the years.

The story is organised in two parallel strands. Firstly the biographic details of Lizzie's life; and secondly, sections that seek to set the context of her life within the wider events that were happening and to help to fill in local detail to add clarity to the narrative.

So, here is the story of Lizzie Watts, born in Victorian times, a loving wife, a mother of a large family and in particular four sons who fought in the Great War, and a survivor who knew hardship and loss but also joy and celebration.

Phil Watts

(Staffordshire 2021)

phil.watts@cantab.net

LIZZIE – MY EARLY DAYS

"I've always seen myself as a fortunate, maybe even a lucky person, particularly around my family, until that night. The fire changed all that forever in ways that I wouldn't wish on anyone. Some pains are worse than dying but life has to go on. But I'm getting ahead of myself, there's a lot to tell before that and stories should be told as they happened as Mother drummed into me, 'There's a right way of telling tales and that's in the order that things happen and not otherwise'. I've lived a long life as measured by some folks' lot. There's much I remember with much fondness and joy but some also with great sadness that I'll never forget. I'm sure there's much that I have forgotten but I hope that these don't affect the telling of my story.

I'm sorry to say that I can't remember too much detail about my very young childhood. Talking now, I do so wished I'd asked Mother more. Sorry to say I didn't and you just don't realise until it's too late. Never mind that now, so here's what I do recall.

One of the cottages at Spratts typical of the locality

My Mother and Father were Emma and Henry – although I never called them that, they were always Mother and Father – never Ma and Pa. We lived in the house at Spratts where Father grew up as a child. They were married in 1857 in Addlestone, at St Paul's Church where we went when we were children.

I was the third child – Mary (1859) and Emma (1861) were my elder sisters, they were 4 and 2 when I was born. When I was very young I thought I had a third sister – Louisa (Halford). Much later I understood that she was a foundling taken in by Mother from a big place in London.

I was only 4 years old when a Lady came to collect Louisa and take her back to London. I was too young to properly understand what was happening then but I do recall how sad everyone was. I was confused and not a little scared that someone would just come and take me away. Later I came to understand how it all worked.

It was close to this time when my first brother James was born. This is maybe my earliest really vivid memory. Mary, Emma and I were sent out to play and told not to come in again until we were called. Mother's yelling and screams of pain are still etched in my mind. We knew she was having a baby and I was only a little comforted by Mary saying, 'It was just like this when you came. At least it's not raining this time.'

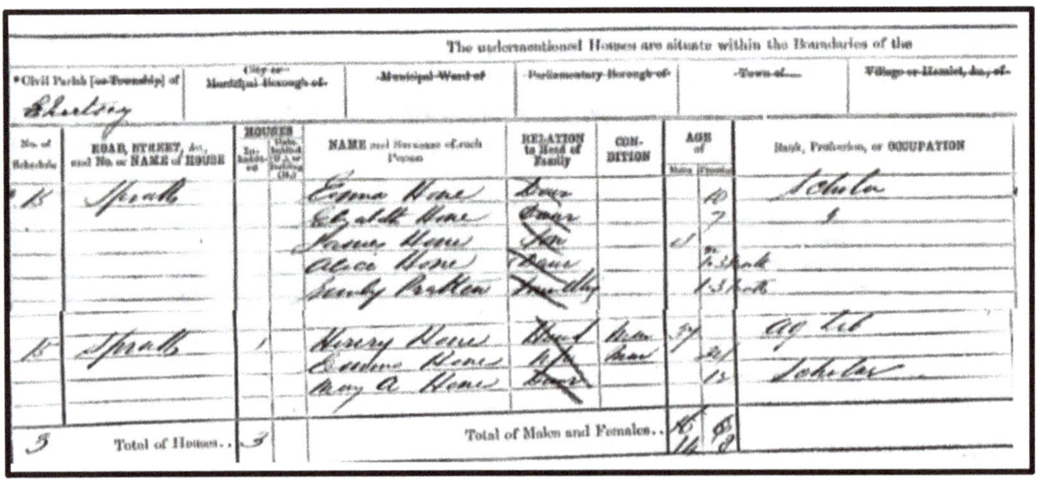
The undermentioned Houses are situate within the Boundaries of the

No. of Schedule	ROAD, STREET, &c., and No. or NAME of HOUSE	HOUSES	NAME and Surname of each Person	RELATION to Head of Family	CONDITION	AGE of Males	AGE of Females	Rank, Profession, or OCCUPATION
	Spratts		Emma Hone	Daur			10	Scholar
			Elizabeth Hone	Daur			7	
			James Hone	Son				
			Alice Hone	Daur				
	Spratts	1	Henry Hone	Head				
			Emma Hone					
			Mary A Hone	Daur			12	Scholar
	Total of Houses		Total of Males and Females					

Extract from 1871 Census recording the Hone Family at that time

I was 7 when Alice was born. I remember it very well as it was just after Christmas and we'd had such a good time, going to Church for the celebration services and having games at home. Very soon we had another 'sister', a foundling from London again – Emily (Pratten). She came just after Alice's christening. Emily stayed with us until she was nearly 5 years old. I remember visits from a very frightening lady asking questions of Mother. Though later I understood that the lady was an inspector from Thomas Corum Hospital checking on Louisa. She used to arrive in a covered carriage drawn by a single horse and driven by a coachman. Oh, it was such a handsome horse, dapple grey and with a wonderful mane. I used to sneak out and stroke it when the coachman was there. Father called it a Broom Carriage, something that confused me because I couldn't see any brushes. Later I learned that the lady came from one of the big houses the other side of the crossroads with the Guildford Road and the proper name of the carriage was a Brougham. You said it 'Broom'. No wonder I was confused.

Mother was always careful to make sure the cottage was tidy before the visits. It was clearly something special. It's not that we didn't have visitors; the neighbours were always dropping in for this and that. This was clearly something important. The lady seemed to be very scary and formal asking lots of questions and looked around the cottage. I didn't hear everything that was happening but tried to listen as best I could! We were all so sad when they came to collect our Emily. I couldn't believe that I might never see her again. It affected us all very hard. I think I would have been around 12 years old at the time.

It affected us all very hard as Emily had been placed to be with Alice so that Mother could nurse them both. But tragedy struck our family. The very next year baby Alice was taken ill and died in the October. We were devastated. She was only 18 months old and just started to toddle and to say a few words. I remember Mother trying to comfort us by saying that 'She's at peace now with God in Heaven.' It seemed little to soothe the hurt and loss we all felt. She had been such a happy baby, always with a smile and a gurgle, rarely crying but easily comforted. It was my first experience of losing someone you loved. There was talk of whether Emily would have to go back to London but Mother and Father made their views clear. 'She's been abandoned once in her short life, it's not going to happen again.' With Alice gone, Emily was doted on by all of us children, you might even say she was spoilt, but we were just giving her the love that Alice would have had. I think it was our way of trying to make things right.

It was around this time that I remember Mother and Father taking all of us down into Addlestone to hear a 'great man preach' at the Crouch Oak. The oak was famous locally as it was so old and absolutely enormous, over twenty feet around and hollow inside. Local legend was that Queen Elizabeth I once picnicked there as the tree used to mark the edge of Windsor Forest where the Kings of England would hunt in olden days. Sometimes we used to play at the oak after school. All I really recall about the preaching was a man with a booming voice talking at a huge crowd for what seemed like hours. When I was older Mother would sometimes talk about this event in reverent tones calling the preacher, Charles Spurgeon, one of God's wonders.

Charles Spurgeon (1834-1892) Baptist Preacher

The last of the family to arrive was Lawrence in 1875 when I was 12 years old – so altogether there were five of us children. We lived in a little cottage in Spratts in an area called Ottershaw, on the outskirts of Chertsey. It was the house where Father's father (Grandpa William) had lived before he moved to nearby Brox. The house was always very lively but there were also many other children to play out with from nearby.

We always loved it when Grandpa William came to visit – it usually meant we had newly soled shoes or even a new pair because he was a shoemaker – so we never wanted for good shoes all the time we all were growing up even if they had been passed down from an older sister. We were so lucky as some of our friends were often barefoot other than Sundays for church of course. Grandpa died when I was just 9 years old. Our shoes were never the same after that but we missed him most because he was so kind to us all.

We didn't see Mother's father - Grandpa John, very often because he lived in London. It was a big event when he came down. We'd all walk down to the station and meet him off the train. We would all walk back on his favourite route – turn right at the Dukes Head, stop at the Holly Tree for him to have an ale and then walk down Simplemarsh and up School Lane to the Church to visit Grandma Mary's grave before going home up the hill. He also used to live in Spratts when he was much younger and before Grandma Mary died – I never knew her 'cos she had died a long time before I was born.

We were lucky as children as there was a nearby school which we all went to – well until we were 11 or 12 years old. St Paul's school was behind the church. This was about a 15 minute walk, if we hurried so as not to be late for school or church. Mother and Father were always very firm on us all going to school and learning to read and write properly. Mother could read and write but Father could do neither, just like Grandpa William, but he wanted us all to have the advantage of learning.

St Paul's Church Addlestone - The school was behind the church, around the corner in School Lane where the teachers lived on site in two cottages

When I was growing up there were always lots of children to play with at Spratts. Just up the row were George and Joseph, they were the Curtis's, both a little older than me but they played with Mary and Emma; Sarah at number 20 was a good friend and my age, along with Alice Emery at number 24. There was always someone from the Russells at number 13 – Henry, George, William, Edward, James, Kate or baby Albert – a real house full, just like us. Best fun of all though, were the Butler twins next door – Stephen and Ernest, who were my age and in the same class at school. They were so alike that I'm sure even Mrs Butler got them confused at times – the teacher in school certainly did! She often insisted that they wore some distinguishing item like a scarf or ribbon but sometimes the twins swopped them over - and then often got the cane for their antics!

School was very strict and could be painful if you misbehaved or got things wrong. The teacher's cane was used most days although more boys got 'six strokes' than us girls, but we weren't spared it if teacher thought we deserved it – whether we agreed or not! Woe betides you if you cried when you got the cane. Oft as not you got an extra stroke for making a fuss. You soon learned how to keep quiet and bite your lip to stop the tears.

Father worked at one of the nurseries nearby where they grew vegetables and flowers. They used to send these up to Covent Garden in London several times a week by horse and cart. Sometimes the flowers were sent by train from the station in town. Something was happening all through the year but the busiest time of all was the harvest. All the men worked in the fields even if it was not the farm they usually worked on. After the corn was taken away, Mother and us children used to go gleaning – picking up whatever corn had been missed from the sheaths. Mother said this was really important as the gleanings made enough flour to keep us in bread for some of the winter. Other times we might help out weeding the fields when the corn was growing. The men used to say it was easier for us children to do this as we were closer to the weeds!

Just round the corner of our row of cottages was the pottery and they used to get their clay from the old clay pit opposite – we weren't supposed to play there because of the water and the deep pit, but we did sometimes. The pottery was mostly a family business but some other men worked there when they were very busy. The horse and cart from Chertsey came once a week to pick up the newly made pottery and take it off for sale. It was fascinating watching them load all the vases, flowerpots and the huge rhubarb pots that looked like they had little hats on. They were all packed with straw so that they didn't get broken on the rough road back to town.

Typical Rhubarb Pots

Other men in the area used to work at the Ongar Hill brickworks which were just a short walk away. That had its own clay pit too but this was fenced off and they didn't like children playing near there.

We were lucky in having one of the bigger gardens of the cottages at Spratts and we could grow a lot of our own vegetables. We all had to help out with tending the crops, weeding, and getting water from the well when it hadn't rained.

Overall I'd say I had a happy childhood. Sometimes food was short and we might be hungry but Mother always found ways of making that up when there was more available and we might have special treats. We all got on well as brothers and sisters. True we fell out and squabbled but we soon made it up again. Looking back now, it seemed all too soon that I was about to leave school and start work.

Were they the best years of my life? Maybe, because I had so few responsibilities and worries but I had great joys to come too with my own family later. Sometimes I wish I had some photographs from that time but they were very rare then and very expensive. We simply couldn't afford them. The oldest photo I have is of Syd's father, Henry. He had a very impressive beard! It's a shame I don't have any of my own dear Mother and Father but I have their images in my head."

Henry Watts (1817 – 1899)

SPRATTS AND OTTERSHAW

The earliest settlement in Ottershaw was along the Bourne stream near to Dunford Bridge, and by the Tudor period there were also a few scattered farms nearby. Ottershaw formed part of the ancient parish of Chertsey, an old market town to the south west of London and situated in the county of Surrey.

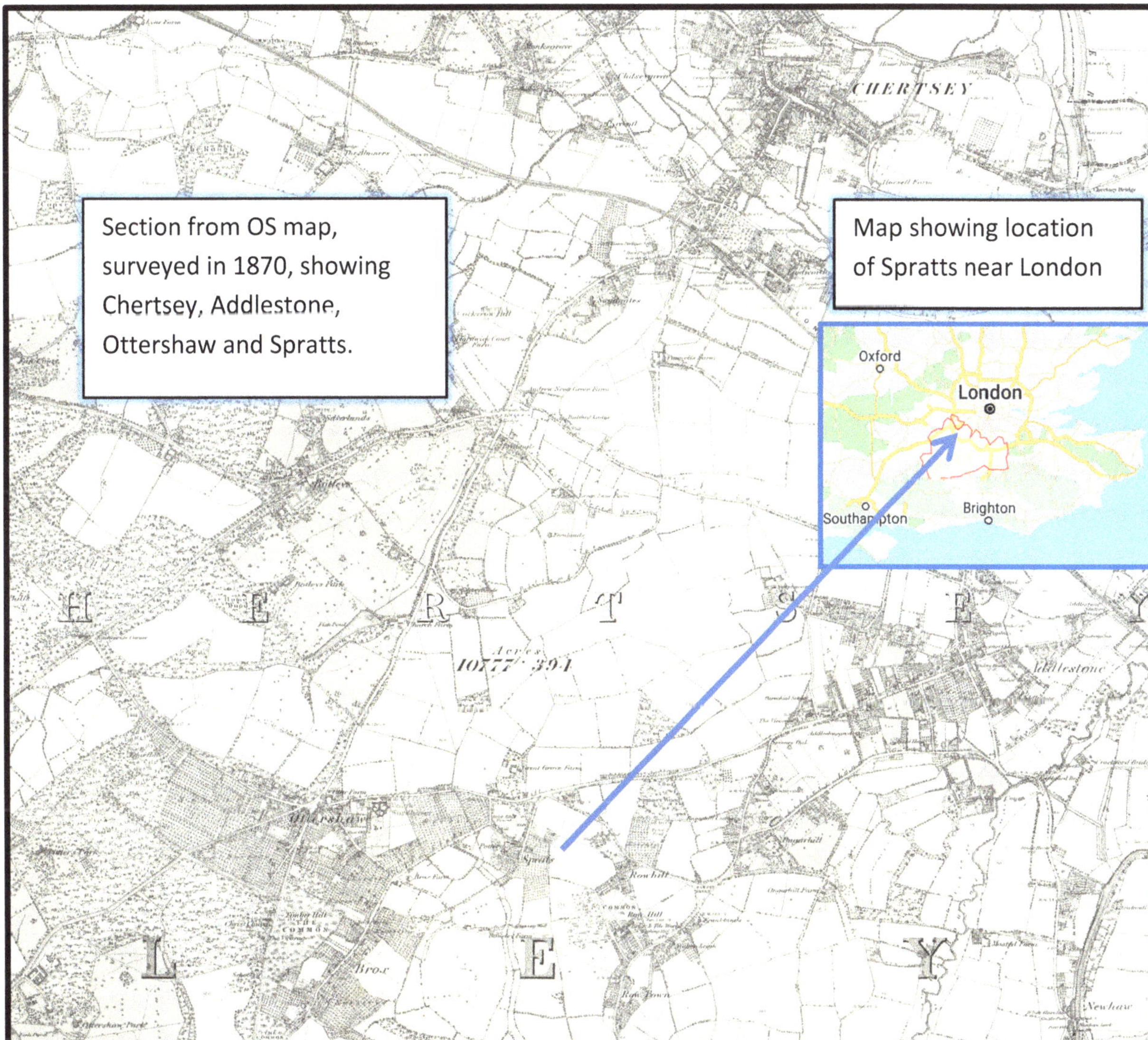

Section from OS map, surveyed in 1870, showing Chertsey, Addlestone, Ottershaw and Spratts.

Map showing location of Spratts near London

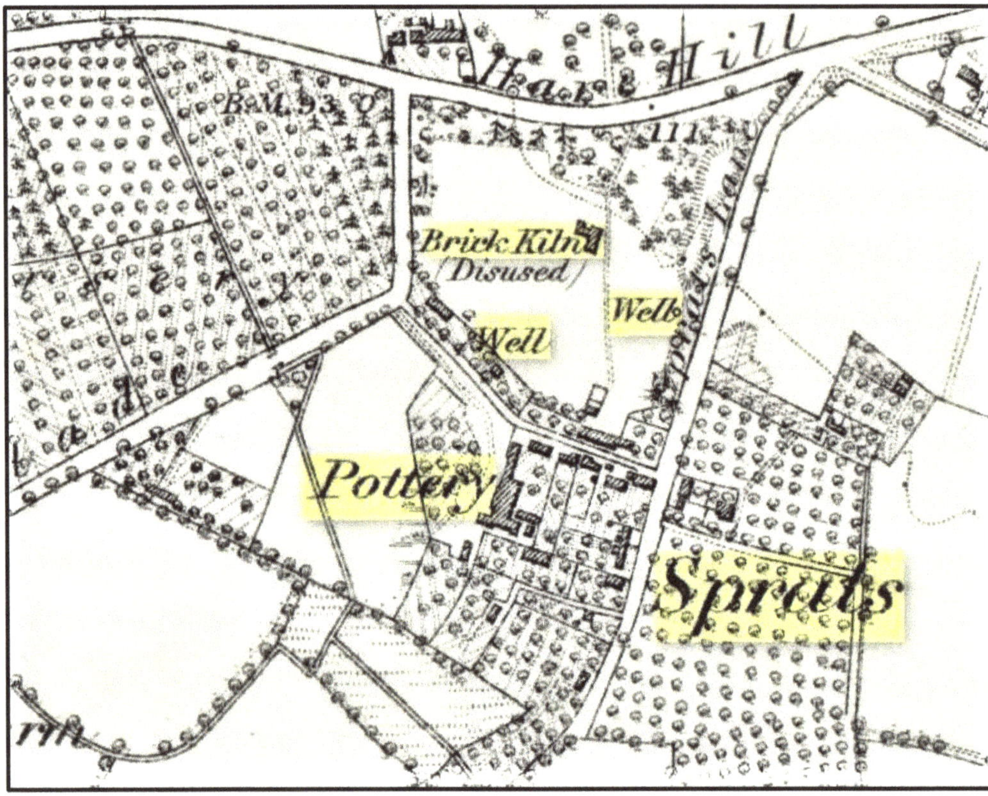

Close up map (1870) showing the detail of the Spratts area
Includes the Pottery, Brick Kiln, wells and individual cottages

During the 16th century several small farms were established in the wasteland including Brox, Bousley, Potters Park and Spratts. These remained as farms until the 19th century when they became nurseries supplying vegetables and cut flowers to London. The daily journey to Covent Garden could just be made by horse and cart. The two farms of an earlier date, Anningsley and Ottershaw, came under more wealthy lessees from London in the 16th and 17th centuries, who rebuilt them as their country houses and parks, as well as continuing as farms.

Ottershaw Park around 1900-1905

It was not until the mid-19th century that the name of Ottershaw, from the estate of that name, came into general use as the village name. At this time Sir Edward Colebrook, owner of Ottershaw Park, provided the land and paid for the fine church, whose architect was Sir Gilbert Scott. Ottershaw would later became recognised as a parish separate to Chertsey.

The nearest school was St Paul's in Addlestone until Sir Edward paid for the building of Junior and Infant schools on Guildford Road. In 1870 they opened as one school, run by the Church of England, but school records show there was frequent absenteeism. Reasons for this are given as going to local fairs, circuses and working as beaters in local shoots. The local agricultural economy also relied on the work of children, and so there were often absentees for seasonal activities. These included the acorn and chestnut harvest in November, plus furze collecting for the bonfire in November, as well as hay and corn harvests, and fruit and mangel-wurzel picking in summer.

The labourers mostly lived in small daub/stone cottages in the three hamlets of Brox, Spratts and Chertsey End Lane. These often had to be rebuilt and there is now little remaining of the old houses in this area of Ottershaw.

Apart from work on the estates of these large houses, many local people were employed in the nursery gardens, which were established in the Ottershaw area around 1820 and continued there until the 1930s. The local clay was also good for brick-making, tiles and pottery and there were works in the area from around 1777. Bonsey's Pottery was founded about 1851 and made a large range of items including flowerpots, vases, ornamental pots, sea kale and rhubarb pots as well as the usual tiles, bricks and garden edging.

THOMAS CORAM – THE FOUNDLING HOSPITAL

Eighteenth century London was a mass of contrasts. A gin-swilling public rubbed shoulders with gentlefolk keen to do good work. In the early decades of the eighteenth century, children were dying at an alarming rate after decades of severe epidemics (typhus, dysentery, measles, and influenza). The Gin Craze was in full swing with disastrous effects, as famously captured by the contemporary artist Hogarth. At the time it was estimated that in London gin consumption was around seven gallons per adult per year. One of the tragic consequences was large numbers of very young children being either entirely abandoned or thrown upon the mercies of the parish, sometimes being handed over to parish officers for a lump sum.

Nationally, the only provision for illegitimate babies was the parish poorhouse or workhouse where young children frequently died of neglect. Mortality rates were extremely high - in London three quarters died before they were five. In workhouses the death rate could be as high as 90%.

The Thomas Coram Foundling Hospital was one product of the great wave of philanthropic activity that took place in England during the eighteenth century. Sea Captain Thomas Coram retired to Rotherhithe in 1719 after achieving much success in the colonies of America. He had established a shipwright's business in Boston, and then later in Taunton, Massachusetts

A frequent early morning walker, Coram was appalled at the sight of dead and dying babies abandoned on the streets. This spurred him into action. Initially, his idea was to petition the king for a charter to create a non-profit-making organisation supported by subscriptions. At first this met with no success because he was unable to find anyone influential enough to approach the King. There was opposition to such an idea because some thought that it might encourage wantonness and loose living.

Coram finally had success after King George I died in 1727. Queen Caroline, wife of the new King George II, was sympathetic to the fate of foundlings. In 1739, after presenting numerous petitions which emphasised both Coram's compassion for the children and the desire to turn them into useful citizens, the King signed a Royal Charter. On 20th November 1739, the Governors and Guardians of this new enterprise met to receive the Charter at Somerset House to establish the Thomas Coram Foundling Hospital for the 'education and maintenance of exposed and deserted young children.'

A site was found in the area known as Bloomsbury Fields, the Earl of Salisbury's estate, lying north of Great Ormond Street. The Earl donated £500 of the £7000 needed for the development. This institution, described as 'the most imposing single monument erected by eighteenth century benevolence', caught the public imagination and became London's most popular charity.

William Hogarth, the artist, had a long association with the Hospital and was a founding Governor. He designed the children's uniforms, the Coat of Arms and he and his wife Jane fostered foundling children. Hogarth also decorated the walls of the hospital with works of art. His example led to many other contemporary British artists donating works including Sir Joshua Reynolds, Thomas Gainsborough, Richard Wilson and Francis Hayman. At this time Britain had no public places for artists to exhibit their works and the Foundling Hospital became what was to be the first contemporary gallery of British art.

Thomas Coram Hospital Bloomsbury Fields c1900

George Frederic Handel also supported the Hospital's charitable work by giving a benefit performance of his work in the Hospital Chapel. This was such a success that he subsequently gave an annual performance of the Messiah there and later bequeathed a full copy of the score to the Hospital which is still there to this day in the museum.

The first children were admitted to the hospital in 1741. At that time the concept of the word 'hospital' implied the hospitality shown to children in their care, rather than a place for the sick.

Mothers brought their babies to the Hospital, where the infants would be given a new name and identity. However, mothers left personal tokens with the hospital so that the child could be identified if the mother subsequently enquired about or wanted to claim her child. These tokens might be a card, a coin, a button, a lock of hair, a letter that enabled the identification of the mother and the child. A range of these tokens are also preserved in the museum at Thomas Corum today.

Children had to be less than 12 months of age, and were only admitted after the mother had been interviewed and seen to meet the hospital criteria. Once they had been accepted, children were registered, and were sent to live with a 'nurse' or foster family in the country, usually the Home Counties. While they were fostered, there was a system of home inspection and reporting to ensure their welfare. This was usually carried out by local clergy or the gentry.

The mother was given a Certificate of the reception of the Child, with a private mark upon it. By producing this she could always find out whether the child was still alive, his/her health and the last Report from the Inspectors in the country. There was a careful system of registration, and each child was assigned a number that allowed the tracking and unique identification of the child at any time.

When they reached four or five years of age, children were returned from their foster families to live in residence at the Foundling Hospital in London. Here they received schooling to make sure that both boys and girls were literate and numerate and were able to assist in the day to day running of the hospital in the kitchen or the laundry or elsewhere. When they were 15 years old they were then found apprenticeships, usually to work in domestic or military service.

Louisa Halford, who was placed with Lizzie Hone and her family in 1861, stayed with the family until 1866. Lizzie would only have vague memories of her as she was only 3 or 4 years old when Louisa returned to the Foundling Hospital. Her memories may well be those from other members of the family. The next trace of Louisa is in the 1871 census where she is listed as being a scholar at the Foundling Hospital. Ten years later, at the age of 20, she is living in Norwood near Lambeth in London and working as a domestic parlour maid in the house of Major Samuel B Faddy of the Bengal Infantry (Aged 64, Retired). Maj. Faddy's wife, Eliza, was twenty years younger and they had five children ranging in ages from 9 to 22. Louisa was one of four servants in the house.

The next record of Louisa is her marriage in 1884 to William Tennant, a painter at St Luke's Church, Norwood. The last known record of Louisa, in 1891, shows that she and her husband were living at 27 Ernest Street, Norwood in 1891.

Emily Pratton, who was placed with the Hones when Lizzie was 8 years old, returned to Thomas Coram Hospital in 1876. The next trace of her is in the 1881 census where she is also listed as a scholar in the returns for the Hospital. The last known listing for Emily is in the 1891 census. Here she is listed as a nurse for Leslie Wormald aged 7 months. Leslie's parents were John and Eleanor Wormald and they lived in apartment 4D in the Mansions, Earl's Court Road, Kensington – a very impressive building which still stands today. John is recorded as being the Managing Director of a company manufacturing fire engines. This is thought to be the London branch of Mather and Platt, a company based in Manchester that evolved into a large multi-national engineering company. His younger brothers, Joseph and Henry, emigrated to Australia where they founded a fire prevention and security company. A century after its foundation, Wormald International Ltd had become a world leader in the fire protection and security industry.

At least in these two cases, it would appear from the records that the aims of Thomas Coram and the Foundling Hospital that he established were successfully met. As babies abandoned or 'given up' by their parents, Louisa and Emily received care and education and were then able to make their own way in the world.

LIZZIE - LEAVING HOME

"When I left school at twelve, I could read and write and my arithmetic was good – nearly the best in the class according to my teacher. For the next two years or so I helped out on the farm nearby, as all of us who were of an age had to have a job to help keep the family going. It was hard work and also seasonal, with fruit and mangel-wurzel picking in summer, helping with the harvest in September and then acorn and chestnut harvests in November – oh it got so cold in the woods and then there were all the prickles on the chestnuts, my fingers always bled despite my woollen gloves.

A little later, when I was just 15, Mother heard about a position just down the road in Addlestone for a general housemaid with a retired gentleman in Station Road. I can remember putting on my Sunday best and Mother taking me for an interview. I was very nervous and Mr Taylor seemed to be very stern but his daughter, Eleanor, tried hard to put me at ease. Mr Taylor, as I discovered was a widower, having lost his wife not long after he retired to Addlestone, only a year or so before I started working for the family. He had clearly been an important man, used to giving orders and having them obeyed. I thought it must have been to do with his work in the courts. That all came out a little bit at a time when I was there, mostly it should be said from the part time cook, Vicki. She was a real gossip, always with a tale to tell and usually in a hushed voice. When she used to tell me something, she was always looking over her shoulder almost expecting someone to come in.

I was at first surprised, but then anxious, to find that I was offered the position as it meant that I'd be leaving home and living in. But other girls were doing the same, so I just had to get on with it and not worry about missing my family. After all they weren't that far away and I could see them on my weekly afternoon off that I had been promised.

At the time I was offered the job I didn't know anyone else was living in the house. When I started I found out that much of my everyday work would be set by Mrs Williams, who was a widow. I never really did work out what her relationship was with Mr Taylor but it was often the subject of Vicki's suspicions.

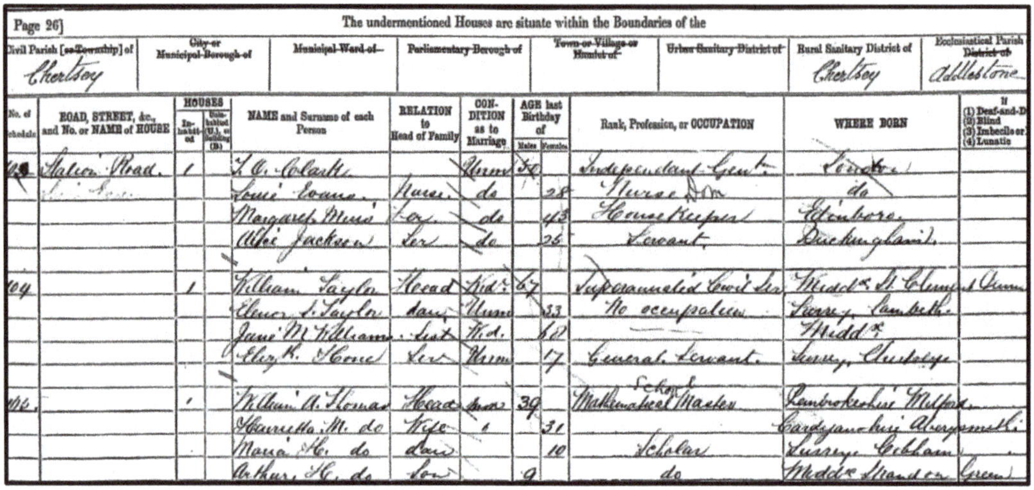

Page 26] The undermentioned Houses are situate within the Boundaries of the

Civil Parish [or Township] of	City or Municipal Borough of	Municipal Ward of	Parliamentary Borough of	Town or Village or Hamlet of	Urban Sanitary District of	Rural Sanitary District of	Ecclesiastical Parish or District of
Chertsey						Chertsey	Addlestone

No. of Schedule	ROAD, STREET, &c., and No. or NAME of HOUSE	HOUSES In-habited	HOUSES Uninhabited (U.), or Building (B.)	NAME and Surname of each Person	RELATION to Head of Family	CONDITION as to Marriage	AGE last Birthday of Males	AGE last Birthday of Females	Rank, Profession, or OCCUPATION	WHERE BORN	(1) Deaf-and-Dumb (2) Blind (3) Imbecile or Idiot (4) Lunatic
103	Station Road	1		T. O. Clarke		Unm	50		Independant Gent	London	
				Louie Evans	Nurse	do		28	Nurse Dom	do	
				Margaret Muir	Ser.	do		43	House Keeper	Edinboro	
				Alice Jackson	Ser	do		25	Servant	Buckinghamshire	
104		1		William Taylor	Head	Wid	67		Superannuated Civil Ser	Middx St Clements	[illegible]
				Eleanor S. Taylor	dau	Unm		33	No occupation	Surrey, Lambeth	
				Jane McWilliam	Sist	Wid.		68	—	Middx	
				Eliz K. Hone	Ser	Unm		17	General Servant	Surrey, Chertsey	
105		1		William A. Thomas	Head	Mar	39		School Mathematical Master	Pembrokeshire Milford	
				Henrietta M. do	Wife	"		31		Cardiganshire Aberystwith	
				Maria H. do	dau			10	Scholar	Surrey, Cobham	
				Arthur H. do	Son		9		do	Middx Strand on Green	

Extract from 1881 Census showing Lizzie working at the Taylors

What did I do? Well looking back, it was a long, long list of duties - lighting the fire, changing bed linens, scrubbing the floor, brushing or cleaning the carpet, beating rugs, washing clothes, making the beds, helping cook, washing the dishes, dusting and cleaning the ornaments, answering the door and announcing visitors – not that there were that many truth to tell. Some days it seemed never ending but then not that different from my life at home. I was lucky compared to some house servants elsewhere in the town. I had my own room, small and in the attic but it was my own room. It was the first time I'd ever slept on my own with only me in the bed. Just that took me some time to get used to – no older sister jabbing me in the ribs or rolling over on top of me, no feet in my face as we sisters all shared a bed and slept top to toe. The attic was small and cold in the winter with only a tiny window and the roof was very low. The furniture was sparse but I had a chair, bed, and a wooden dresser and it was all mine! At first I had to pinch myself to recognise that I was being paid a proper wage in my own right. Mr Taylor was quite generous with my wages after I had proved myself. I received £21 a year and I got a whole afternoon free time each week. Usually this was a Sunday but occasionally this would be changed if there were visitors expected and so I'd have the Wednesday afternoon free. I was always the first to rise in the morning to light the fires and draw the curtains, and often the last to bed although Mr Taylor wasn't one for being late to bed himself.

It wasn't the biggest house in the street but it was warm and welcoming. Next door lived Mr Hennessey, who, I learned, was a Professor of Music. He lived with his wife and their children, including his son John who was a harpist, and also the Governess – Elizabeth, who taught the children at home. It was a busy house as there were always pupils coming and going for piano lessons. After they'd finished you could often hear Mr Hennessey playing some wonderful music especially in the summer when the windows were open. A few times the Taylors were invited round for a recital and thanks to Elizabeth, I got to go too. Oh, how he could play. I'd never heard anything like it before. I believe that's where I got my love of classical music. From then on, I tried not to miss any of the performances of the town band.

Postcard showing Station Road, Addlestone
Mr. Taylor's house on the right hand side in the distance

After I'd been there a while, maybe about three years or so, a new delivery boy bought the groceries from Madeley's in Chertsey. They were the well-known grocers in Windsor Street. I soon learned his name was Sydney, thanks again to Vicki, who told me he was one of the Watts'. They were a well-known family in Chertsey with lots of relatives living in the Windsor Street, Gogmore Lane and Goosepool area. We exchanged an odd word when he bought the groceries in and eventually he asked me if I'd go for a walk one Sunday to hear the local band. I reluctantly agreed as I didn't want to seem too interested. But he was a striking looking lad, just a few months older than me as it turned out. He was quite proud, I never quite knew why, that his birth was registered on New Year's Eve 1862. Maybe he thought that it made him look a year older than if he had been registered a day later?

Anyway, things developed and we started seeing each other regularly. I met his Mother and Father and he met mine. Funnily, both fathers were Henrys and they both worked as gardeners so they had plenty to talk about when they met. Henry Watts was quite successful and Syd once proudly told me he was listed in Kelly's Directory as a Jobbing Gardener along with all the other businesses in town.

Eventually Syd asked me to marry him and we got wed at St Peter's Church on 30th August 1886 when I was 23 years old. Our fathers were the witnesses to the wedding which was quite a big event what with all our relatives living locally. We didn't have far to go for our new home. We had managed to rent a small cottage down Church Walk – it was only about 25 yards from the altar! So close that Syd would often say on a Sunday when the bells were ringing out for morning service, "Where's Blanch Heriot when you need her, so we can have a bit of peace and quiet?" The cottage was all we needed at the time and it was near the centre of the town. We would hear the London stage coach, sometimes two horses but often a four-in-hand, come past the end of the Walk. They would then turn into the courtyard of the Crown right behind our home, followed by all the shouted instructions to the grooms and the baggage boys while they either changed the horses or unloaded the luggage.

Postcard of St. Peter's Church, Chertsey
Entrance to Church Walk is at the side of the church railings behind the lamp post on the right hand side of the picture

Postcard of Crown Hotel and Town Hall
Entrance to the livery stables and coaching inn can be seen on the left hand side foreground

Of course I'd left the employment of Mr. Taylor when I got married. I had worked there nearly eight years. The years had flown by. Later, I heard, they moved just down the way to 136 Station Road, a smaller house but one I thought was probably easier for them to manage now he was in his seventies. Vicki still went in to cook for them and they had a part time maid instead of me. But my life had moved on and I was starting the next stage of my life, one I had always dreamed about – being married and living in my own house.

Maybe I should tell you now about my brothers and sisters and how their lives went. Let me start with my little brothers but they weren't so very little. They grew up to be strapping lads and both of them worked in the market gardens in the Spratts area just like their father. James married Emily in 1890 and they soon had a little baby George. They moved into a cottage down Station Road a little way along from where I worked for the Taylors until they moved back into Spratts a bit later. Laurence didn't marry at first and tried his hand at bricklaying when he moved to Walton to live. Emma married a lovely man called William Dollery and had four children. They were very good supporting mother but more about that later.

All so well and good, so far. Mary, the eldest was the source of a good deal of worry and anger in the family. She had been walking out with another Henry for a good while. This wasn't something that Father was very happy about as Henry was nearly 10 years older and hadn't really settled down. Father was furious when Mary told Mother that she was expecting. I already knew about the baby as Mary had come down to see me at the Taylors and asked me what she should do and how to break the news. I was at a loss as I'd never had to think of anything like that before. She put if off for a while until she couldn't wait any longer. Well, Father was furious, Mother was shocked. It was made all the worse when Father got to know that Henry wasn't planning to marry Mary. He went round to the family house which was on the way to Lyne, only to find that Henry had left according to his father, John. Packed his bags and gone to London. Well, Father was beside himself. When I visited on my afternoon off, the family was in turmoil. Father was seething with rage, Mother was worried about Mary and how the family would cope with the shame if something wasn't resolved. I had never heard my father use such language before. Henry's ears must have been burning red hot. Even Mother, who could usually find something good in anyone, condemned him and said he was on a sure path to Hell. I'd never in my life heard anything like it. It was such a mess and there was nothing I could do except to try and console Mary.

Fortunately it was resolved. Henry came back from London, apologising to everyone, saying he panicked and ran, not knowing what to do, probably hoping it would all go away. But babies don't have a habit of doing that do they? I wasn't there for the meeting of Henry and Father but from what Mother told me it wasn't a pleasant affair but plans were agreed. Anyway they got married at the end of April 1880 and the baby arrived in July. A lovely healthy little girl. They named her Alice after our little sister that we lost all those years ago. It was such a lovely gesture that I determined that if we were blessed with a girl, I too would call her Alice. After all the trouble, shock and anger, you might have hoped that their lives would be smoother from then. But it was not to be. Henry was only 36 when he died six years later, leaving poor Mary to cope on her own."

EMPOYERS AND NEIGHBOURS

The head of the household in Station Road was William Taylor, 64, described as a superannuated civil servant and a widower in the census of 1881. William had been the Chief Clerk to Westminster Police Court for many years and had served there in the early years of the newly formed Metropolitan Police Force which superseded the Bow Street Runners. The policemen in the force being established by Sir Robert Peel were colloquially known as 'Peelers'. William Taylor is first recorded in this role of Chief Clerk in the 1851 census; he and his wife Mary were living in Stockwell at the time. The family were in Hampton Road Twickenham in 1861 and then in Battersea in 1871. The family then moved to Addlestone but not long after, Mary sadly died on 22nd December 1876. By 1891 he had moved again to 136 Station Road, a slightly smaller property.

He would have been a relatively well-off person – the salary for the chief clerk at Bow Street Police Court was £250 in 1835 increasing by £10 per year to £450 (Approx. equivalent £60,000 in 2021) with a good pension. The primary role of the chief clerk was to provide legal advice to magistrates in the court room and in their retiring room on questions of law, practice and procedure, as well as assisting in the administration of the court business.

Station Road was a mixed development within Addlestone. The road was home to a mixture of families, shops and trades. It developed from the Duke's Head crossroads down to the new station in the mid-19th century. The branch line to Weybridge opened in 1848 and local people could travel to London Waterloo by changing trains at Weybridge, only one stop away. The opening of the station also made the transfer of fresh goods to the markets in London much quicker and easier.

Apart from Mr Taylor and Mr Hennessey other residents were labourers, a carpenter, bricklayer, gardeners, a coal merchant and a grocer's assistant. There were also teachers of Music, Mathematics and English as well as a Clerk in the Admiralty. There was a variety of shops including grocers, butchers, boot maker, florist and several inns including the new Railway Inn.

BLANCHE HERRIOT

Blanche Heriot is a legendary tale set in Chertsey at the time of the Wars of the Roses fought between the Royal Houses of Yorkshire and Lancashire. The time is 1471 and Edward IV, the first Yorkist king, has just regained his throne from Henry VI. Blanche is a young woman living in Chertsey and she has a lover, Neville Audley, who has been away fighting in the wars but for the losing Lancastrian side.

Fleeing from the battle at Barnet, he returns to Chertsey with a price on his head but is captured by Yorkist soldiers in Chertsey. He escapes by killing one soldier and seeks sanctuary in Chertsey Abbey, at the time one of the largest and most wealthy abbeys in England. Shockingly, the sanctuary is broken, he is arrested and sentenced to die on the stroke of curfew the following day. Neville has one possible way out. He has a ring previously given to him in thanks by a Yorkist nobleman on the battlefield when Neville spared him his life. His friend, Herrick Evenden agrees to take the ring to the king in London, to call in the favour and plead for Neville's life.

Chertsey Curfew Bell, cast in 1370.

Origin of the poem:

'Curfew Must Not Ring Tonight'

Long, long years I've rung the Curfew

From that gloomy shadowed Tower;

Every evening, just at sunset,

It has told the Twilight hour.

All the next day, Blanche and Neville wait anxiously for Herrick to return. With only a few minutes until the curfew bell is rung, Herrick is seen at Laleham Ferry, more than half a mile away. Knowing that Neville's life depends on her delaying the curfew, Blanche runs to the bell tower, races up the old stairs, crawls under the bell and clings onto the clapper. Despite being battered between bell and frame she doggedly holds on even when the sexton and soldiers climb the tower to see why the bell is not ringing. Just then Herrick arrives clutching a pardon bearing the king's seal. Neville is released, a party is held at a local inn and Blanche and Neville are married shortly afterwards.

This old Chertsey legend was first captured in print as a play by the Victorian writer, Albert Smith in 1842 with great success. The Irish actress Maria Honner played the heroine and her life size portrait was on many hoardings in London, swinging to and fro with her hair streaming in the wind. The story was then picked up and formed the basis of the narrative poem "Curfew Must Not Ring Tonight" by Rose Hartwick Thorpe in 1867 which apparently became a favourite of Queen Victoria. The poem begins:

England's sun was slowly setting o'er the hills so far away,
Filling all the land with beauty at the close of one sad day;
And its last rays kissed the faces of a man and maiden fair,–
He with step so slow and feeble; she with sunny, floating hair;
He with bowed head, sad and thoughtful, she with lips so cold and white,
Firmly set to hush the murmur, "Curfew must not ring to-night."

Opening page of Rose Hartwick Thorpe's poem, published in 1867

More recently, a bronze statue of Blanche Heriot by Sheila Mitchell F.R.B.S was erected near Chertsey Bridge.

LIZZIE – MY EARLY MARRIED LIFE WITH SYD

"We were so happy in our new home together although Syd's hours were long and it was hard work as a porter with Madeley's. His wages weren't generous but it was enough for us to get by on and get the house a bit straight. We then had just the most wonderful Christmas ever. I found I was expecting our first child. Syd was delighted as were all the family. I told him one Sunday when we were taking our usual walk down to Abbey Bridge and onto the Ferry. I remember talking to Mother over Christmas as I didn't know quite what to expect. Although I had seen Mother with all my younger brothers and sister it wasn't the same as having a child yourself. She was, as usual, matter of fact and calm, "Folk have been doing this for ever. It'll be fine. Just take good care of yourself. Just don't go overdoing things late on." And that, I think, was about it for advice. I got more advice from neighbours much later but it all just seemed common sense along with a few old wives' tales which I mostly ignored. As it turned out, there was nothing to worry about. We had a delightful baby boy the following July, good and healthy and bawling his lungs out! He was baptised on 24th July, 1887 it was, by the Reverend Powell who had married us the previous year. We named him Thomas after his grandfather – there were a number of Tom Watts over the years going back, I think, four or five generations.

Turns out, Tom was just the start. We went on to be blessed with 11 children in all – six boys and five girls. Tom was followed by Sydney, born on 21st November, just a year later in 1888, another big bouncy healthy boy.

But I'm racing ahead of myself now, I need to go back a little to just before Tom was born. There was one event that has stuck in my mind all these years and in everyone else's too that experienced it. I must tell you about it and all the details that have stayed with me as fresh as the day they happened - the Golden Jubilee of our Queen, Victoria. Syd and I had only been married a few months and I was heavily expecting with Tom when all the celebrations happened. It was hard for me being so heavy with the new baby but that wasn't going to stop me enjoying the day and all the preparations leading up to it. Oh, what a day! I don't think Chertsey had ever seen anything like it until maybe the Armistice much later. Even the Diamond jubilee, ten years later wasn't as big.

There had been a big committee in the town, led by Mr Webb and Mr Freeman, that had responsibility of organising all the festivities for the Jubilee and what a great job they did too. There was hardly a street that didn't have some connection to the planning and organising. The day passed off without a hitch or at least I noticed none, and it lived in our memories for years. The day of the Jubilee had been declared a national holiday and everyone was determined to enjoy it and make the very best of such a rare occasion. The pubs were certainly busy especially with the celebration Jubilee Ale.

On the Sunday morning before the holiday, a special jubilee service was held at St Peter's. This was a grand affair and the 5th Surrey Rifles marched in formation to the church from the Drill Hall right the way along London Street. The singing of Onward Christian Soldiers was very enthusiastic by both the congregation and thc crowd gathered outside.

The Monday was just mad in the town. It seemed like everyone was busy with decorations for their houses, putting up bunting in the streets, organising lights and lanterns. There was just so much happeninq all at once. So much so that the decorating and preparations went on long into the night. Everyone had really done their all. I'll tell you about some of the decorations in a bit because they really came to life the next day.

Madeley's shopfront

Madeley's shopfront in the early stages of decoration for the Jubilee
Note the VR above the entrance, the flowers and drapes

I remember waking the following morning to a fine sunny May day without any danger of rain to dampen the proceedings. The start of the celebration was signalled by a long peel of bells at 8 o'clock on the Tuesday morning – no chance of us missing that from the cottage! There was a special Thanksgiving Service held half an hour later which was very well attended – the church was full to the brim with loads of folk standing at the back and in the side aisles. The vicar had been very kind and saved me a seat on account of my condition.

Not long after the service, the Grand Procession took place. With all the floats, bands and groups of people it must have been nearly a mile in length. We'd never seen its like before. The procession wound its way through the town, Bridge Rd, up London Street, into Windsor St, round St Anne's Road and South Grove, back into Guildford St and finally down to Guildford Road.

Oh, where to start in describing it all? Most of the tradesmen in the town had a float. Some were even working – Hamiltons were doing copper riveting and pipe bending - all on the move! The brewers and their magnificent drays were there and clearly beer was being drunk! The horses' collars and brasses were polished and shone in the sun. Syd's shop, Madeleys, had a float which was decorated with biscuit tins and a general display of groceries. Syd and a couple of other men had been busy doing this all over the weekend before. There were floats from the coal merchants, the fishmonger, other grocers, the gas company, blacksmith, farmers, milkman, upholsterers and so on as well as the Fire Brigade, the Cricket Club, the Cycling Club, the Anglers – so many I can't remember them all. I do remember the magnificent costumes of the kings and queens through the ages. The old costumes for the Henrys were superb. Henry the Eighth was a magnificent figure. Henry Nesmith, the builder from Guildford Street, had been rightly chosen, with his barrel chest he looked just the part, filling the costume like a true King. And, not forgetting the Army and Navy were represented along with people for the countries of the Empire, Australia, India, Canada and so on.

The bands were spread through the procession and played their hearts out. The Victoria Band and the Rifle Corps Band were there but my favourite were the Drum and Fife players – you could hear them all the way down the street.

After the procession, everyone headed for Botleys where the rest of the day's events were being held. I got a ride on Syd's float as it was too far to walk in my condition. The events were originally to be held at Silverlands but Mr Hankey's second son tragically died only weeks before. So everything was moved to Botleys. The grounds were full of tents, stands, food stalls run by the Crown and the Kings Head, a stage, a running track and a huge marquee had been erected for the celebration lunch for the aged and others. I was told that it sat nearly 400 folk for the lunch. The centrepiece was the roasting of the fattened bullock that had been presented by Captain Norton. There was a toast to the Queen and the National Anthem was sung before the meal.

In the afternoon there were pony races for prizes, a donkey race and athletics events including an obstacle race and climbing the greasy pole for a leg of mutton. Henry Smith, now he lived down Station Road if I remember right, well he won that, to his great delight. On the stage there were variety acts, singing, juggling, a tight wire walker, trapeze artist and very strangely, performing goats! Afterwards there was dancing to the music of the bands.

Things came to a close roundabout eight o'clock with another rousing singing of the National Anthem. Then everyone made a move back down to the town to look at the decorations which were simply amazing. At nine o'clock all the illuminations were lit and the town sparkled with what looked like thousands of lights and lanterns.

Syd and I just quietly wandered through the town drinking in the all the sights. There were flags, bunting, Chinese lanterns, floral decorations, and VR on many buildings in fabric or flowers or painted signs. I particularly remember Mr Blaney, you'll remember, the plumber and decorator down Windsor Street, had a sign saying England's Glory with a huge crown underneath. It was very impressive and must have taken so much time and effort. There were other signs saying Long Live the Queen or Queen of Queens. Mr Tulk, at Cowley House, had flags and scarlet drapery with white ribbon and blue rosettes. Mr Stott's house and shop, by Bell Corner, had a huge flag with a portrait of the Queen in the centre and surrounded by evergreen sprigs and fairy lights – just wonderful!

As we walked slowly back towards home through the crowds, we saw Herring and Sons had a display in gas lights – we had never seen them used like that before. Eventually we got home, excited but exhausted from the long day that had been such a triumph for the town. I'll never forget the sights and sounds of that day, the whole town coming together as one to celebrate our Queen.

Getting back to the family again, there was less to celebrate. We had a terrible winter when little Sydie was two years old. Awful frosts and no end of snow, it seemed to go on for ever. The house was so difficult to keep warm with two young children and as for getting the washing dry, well it just froze on the line. It was so cold that the River Thames froze over – something that hadn't happened in two generations. I well recall walking out one Sunday with Syd and the two children, going down Abbey path out to the ferry at Laleham, where instead of the boat across to the Shepperton side we just walked. Well, I say walked, we tottered, slid and fell across. There were folk skating and sliding, having such great fun. Someone had lit a big fire and were roasting meats, chestnuts, potatoes and generally doing a great trade. At some time in the spring, it finally got warm again and the daffodils and snowdrops came out up St Anne's Hill, and finally winter was over.

In 1893, Edith was born, followed quickly by Henry who was born on 27th June 1894. But I'm getting a bit ahead of myself now as there were other things happening that I need to tell you about.

First we had the chance of a bit bigger cottage in Grove Road near Syd's parents who lived at 109. Number 102 was to be home for us all for the next few years. It was much newer than Church Walk and gave us a bigger garden to grow some vegetables. At first this seemed ideal but it turned out to be tragically bad timing.

That autumn, 1894, I remember it so clearly, it was wet beyond belief. It just rained and rained. Eventually the inevitable happened and the Thames broke its banks along with the Bourne. It wasn't the first time the town had been flooded. There'd been floods back in 1875 but nothing like this. A lot of Chertsey flooded – Guildford Street, Windsor Street, Bridge Road, Stepgates, St Anne's - and Grove Road too.

Floods in Grove Road
1894

We had to move what we could upstairs and live there. We got about by boat into town on a couple of days when the flood was at its height. Other times we tried to wade. The floods peaked on 17th November, they said afterwards. They were so bad that some places were isolated like little islands like Wraysbury and Runnymead. It was so unlucky as it turned out – our move I mean. If only we'd stayed in Church Walk another few months we'd have been alright and saved all the trouble. The church was the highest point in the town and never flooded at all! The papers called it the greatest flood ever and the Thames was at 10 feet above its right level. Thousands were driven from their homes. Windsor was badly affected and it was said that the Queen herself gave money for the flood relief. The papers said that in some parts the Thames was more than two miles wide!

Floods in Guildford Street 1894

Eventually the water went but it left such a mess. The mud was everywhere, it seemed like we were cleaning for weeks. But everyone pulled together 'cos it was the same for all. We just couldn't dry the cottage out, the plaster and the floorboards downstairs were sodden, all our clothes felt and smelled of damp no matter what I did. It seemed it couldn't get worse but it did. From New Year's Eve through to March it was so cold, with snow and very hard frosts almost every night. The Thames was blocked in London by ice flows. I got a postcard from my cousin, another Lizzie, describing this. It sounded awful. Afterwards the papers called it the 'twelve week frost'. For weeks it never seemed to get above freezing and it was so hard just to keep one room warm.

It was about this time that little Henry got ill. It started with a fever and then he couldn't keep my milk or anything down. Whatever I got into him never stayed. I made soups, soft foods, bread and milk but nothing helped. He lost weight over time, we had the doctor in but his remedies did nothing. I nursed him day and night but at the end there was nothing of him. The doctor said it was marasmus on the death certificate – or acute malnutrition as he explained. Henry had just wasted away unable to take any goodness from his food. We were distraught. I hadn't lost anyone since little Alice when I was just a child. I blame the flood and the winter. It was so hard on a little baby and he just couldn't hold on for the warmer weather. He died on the 4th of April and with many tears and much sadness, we buried him in Eastworth Road cemetery.

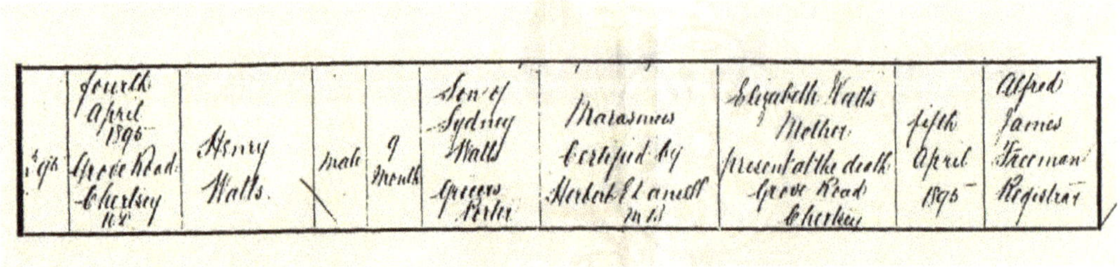

198	fourth April 1895 Grove Road Chertsey U.D.	Henry Watts	male	9 months	Son of Sydney Watts Greens Porter	Marasmus Certified by Herbert Barnett M.R.	Elizabeth Watts Mother Present at the death Grove Road Chertsey	fifth April 1895	Alfred James Freeman Registrar	

Death Certificate for Henry Watts 1895

No matter how hard, life seems to go on even if you think you can't. In no time I found I was expecting again, maybe God's way of compensating for losing Henry. I don't know, it was with mixed feelings I faced this new pregnancy. Anyway, all went well and it was a son. Albert was born on 26th Jan 1896 and was baptised on 8th March 1896 by the Reverend Parr at St Peter's.

Life just seems to one big seesaw of ups and downs. Only two years later, when I was 35 my father Henry passed away in 1898 at the age of 63. Mother was able to carry on living at Sprats on her own for a while but later her grandson Roland came to live with her. Roland had been tragically widowed early in his marriage and he moved in with his sisters Nora and Lois. They helped out and generally made it easier for Mother to cope.

The Lord giveth and taketh away it seems for soon I was expecting again. Clara Beatrice was born in 1897 in Chertsey, Surrey, followed the next year by Fredrick Oliver. It seemed like I was always expecting.

The next year we moved just down the road to number 19 Grove Road. We needed the space now that we had six children and to tell the truth I wasn't sorry to leave a house that reminded me so much of the death of little Henry. The new cottage at number 19 was just a bit more comfortable and warmer too. Now we had gas provided by the gasworks that were just over the Station. We had lights and a gas fire too. No more eking out the candles to make them last the evening.

ARRIVAL OF REFUGEES AND POWs

In October 1914, all non-nationals or 'aliens' (as they were referred to at that time) in Chertsey and elsewhere in the Borough, were rounded up and taken to a detention camp in Frimley under DORA, the Defence of the Realm Act. Later in the war these internees, together with German prisoners of war, would be transported daily from the camps to farms across the area to help with the sowing and harvesting of crops.

The war displaced many hundreds of thousands of people including people from Belgium who fled the advancing German army. By early October 1914, Belgian refugees were being housed across the area and residents were encouraged to give up their spare rooms to those requiring housing.

LIZZIE – TOM, MY ELDEST

"Now I can start telling you about my four lads, my darling, brave lads. They never hesitated to do their duty and at least one of them was too quick off the mark - but more about that later. Tom was my eldest and always a sensible lad with a calm and unflustered way about him. He never minded taking his turn in looking after his younger brothers and sisters. He was particularly affected and quite beside himself when little Henry died that awful winter back in 1895.

Syd Watts with son Tom and grandson Eric
Late 1914

Tom did well enough at school and when he left, he got a job as an apprentice at the bakers on the corner of Stepgates and Fordwater Road and did really well at it. This was hard work with very early starts in the morning getting all the bread baked - they supplied a number of the shops in Chertsey. He and Violet got married in 1911 and little Eric arrived in 1913. They rented a nice little cottage in Gogmore Lane. This was just up the lane from Herring's Foundry. Now that was a busy place in Chertsey, they had around 100 men working there. Noisy too, so I don't think Tom and Violet got much peace when the foundry was running, which of course was most of the time. Everyone used to shut their windows when the furnace started up as it always bellowed out black smoke to begin with. Heaven help you if you left your washing out on the line! Later, during the War, they moved to 34 Windsor Street right opposite the Cedars where our doctor, Dr. Graham-Hodgson lived. He was known locally to everyone as Dr. H. Sadly his eldest lad, George, was killed in the war.

Tom also joined the police force as a special constable, only part time, mind. He had his successes. While Syd was working for Mr Madeley in Windsor Street, Tom caught a man filching rhubarb from old man Madeley's garden. This even made the local newspaper just before he was mobilised into the Forces. I remember Sydie saying that Mr. Madeley said to him that he was pleased that Tom was so efficient as his rhubarb was one of his great pleasures.

> **THEFT OF RHUBARB.** — Harry George Talbot, labourer, Chertsey, was summoned for stealing a quantity of rhubarb, valued at 6d., growing in a garden belonging to Mr. H. J. Madeley, at Gogmore, Chertsey.—Special Constable Watts said he caught the defendant leaving Mr. Madeley's garden with the rhubarb. He was without his boots.—Fined 19s. 6d., and the Special Constable was commended for his smart capture.

Report in Surrey Advertiser
May 1916

When war was declared, Tom was 27 year old and well settled. I remember the conversations we had with him at that time. He was certain in his mind that he should join up and 'do his bit'. It was so hard as I knew what would happen next. If Tom went,

Syd and Albert wouldn't be far behind as they always looked up to their elder brother in most things. It seemed an awful wrench especially as their second child, Stanley, arrived on 24th May 1915. I well remember one of our 'round the table' family talks where Syd and Albert argued that they should be the first to volunteer as they weren't married and had no children. Albert jokingly said that it'll all be over if we volunteer, and then Tom won't have to go – "You can look after your loaves!" Tom reluctantly agreed and so Syd and Albert were the first to go. As ever though, Tom wasn't for turning and he signed up for the army reserve on 6th December 1915. He was mobilized in May 1916 at Aldershot and was fully enlisted in June 1916.

Maybe because of his experience as a special constable, he was put in the Military Mounted Police and quickly promoted to Lance Corporal. At first Syd and I were a bit relieved, maybe thinking that they wouldn't be right on the front line and maybe a bit safer – how wrong we were! He left for France from Southampton on 16th October and arrived in Rouen the following day. The first letter he sent, he didn't give too many details. But in his later letters, he always tried to sound cheerful, though we could never have imagined the conditions they were all living in.

One of Tom Watts' embroidered postcards home.
Sent December 1917

Tom was always a great letter writer, as was Albert too, and we got frequent letters or postcards from him. I loved the embroidered cards that he sent on occasions. I've still got some of them, they made such precious memories. I learned later that they were made by young girls in France and then sold to the soldiers. They were always so colourful and such a delight to receive.

Tom was always a hardworking and conscientious man and this must have been recognised as later he got another promotion, this time to a full corporal. It came as a terrible shock to receive a card from him saying that he had been wounded. But this was quickly followed by relief that it wasn't the worst news that so many families had sadly been told. He told us that he had been evacuated to the field hospital at Dannes Camiers, very close to the coast near Boulogne. Fortunately we were able to borrow an atlas from one Syd's customers so we could see just where Tom was. He described it as a field hospital with everyone in tents but at least it was quiet and away from the front and the shelling. He was so lucky it wasn't worse and he made a good recovery but was soon posted back to his unit. All our worries just started again.

Part of the field hospital at Dannes Camiers France

He did finally get some short home leave in June 1918, coming home at the same time as Albert. He'd been away and in France for 20 months without home leave. Having him home was a great relief for me at that awful time, but I'll tell you about all of that later.

In the last year of the war, Tom was serving near St Ligier and there was some reporting in the papers about the action in this area. It seemed to go backwards and forwards for weeks. Then we heard from him that he had been awarded the DCM for his efforts. I was so proud. The citation was reported in the paper and I made sure to get a copy and kept it safe for when he returned.

> P/3155 L./C. T. Watts, M.M.P., attd. H.Q., 34th Div. (Chertsey) (LG 3 Sept. 1919).
>
> For consistent devotion to duty during the period 26th Feb. to 16th Sept. 1918, and particularly at St. Leger, during the enemy attack in March, where he did most valuable work in collecting stragglers and assisting wounded, while in charge of three straggler posts. The cool courage, judgment and endurance which he displayed on this and other occasions under heavy shell fire have been most marked.

The official notice of his DCM was reported in the New Year Edition of the London Gazette and again I made sure I had a copy although Tom wasn't one for making a fuss. "I was only doing my duty, same as many others", was his familiar line. He was finally demobbed on 19th April 1919. His DCM was finally awarded in October 1919 and although he didn't qualify for a pension for his DCM, he was awarded a gratuity of £20.

After the war he didn't go back to his job in the bakery but decided to join the police full time. Understandable after all his experience in the War and the prospects were much better. About 18 months later he and the family moved to 16 Albion Road, Twickenham near where Tom was stationed. Some matters with army weren't sorted out by then, and he even had to write to the army requesting them to send his medals there as he hadn't received them by the time he left Chertsey."

Corporal Tom Watts DCM.
Wearing his DCM ribbon on his uniform.
Photographed on his return to England after nearly 2 years in France.

To:- Mr. T. Watts., (P. 3155).
34, Windsor Street,
Chertsey,
Surrey.

Reference your communication dated the 20th. inst:.

Herewith your Certificate of Transfer to Class "Z" Army Reserve returned amended, please acknowledge receipt hereon, stamped addressed envelope enclosed.

Capt. for

Aldershot.
21/5/19.

Officer i/c Records.
Military Police Corps.

Sir
A.O.Z.21 to hand T. Watts

Confirmation of Tom's discharge from the Military Police and transfer to Army Reserve (above)
Tom's letter requesting missing medals due to him (below)

P315[illegible]

76 Albion Road
Twickenham
Middlesex.

To O/C Charge of Records
M. M. Police

Sir
Having changed my address will you kindly forward B.W. Medal & Victory Medal which are due to me to the above address.

Yr Obedt
Thomas Watts D.C.M.
Late L/Cpl P3153 M. M. Police.

Late address
34 Windsor Street
Chertsey Surrey.

[illegible].1.21.

MOUNTED MILITARY POLICE AND GALLANTRY MEDAL

The Royal Military Police (RMP) is the corps of the British Army responsible for the policing of army service personnel. They provide a military police presence both in the UK and while service personnel are deployed overseas on operations and exercises. Members of the RMP were often known as 'Redcaps' because of the scarlet covers on their peaked caps, and their scarlet coloured berets.

The RMP's origins can be traced back to the 13th century with the post of Provost Marshall. In 1685 the role of Provost Marshal General became a permanent post. The Cavalry Staff Corps of the early 19th century is regarded as Britain's first standing military police force and a forerunner of the Royal Military Police. At the outbreak of war, they were known as the Mounted Military Police (MMP).

In 1914 the Mounted Military Police had a total establishment of nearly 5000 men. This number was to grow to around 25000 by the end of the war. When the British Expeditionary Force (BEF) was sent to France in that year, each division had one Assistant Provost Marshal having the rank of Major as well as several Non-Commissioned Officers (NCOs).

The MMP in WW1 dealt with the maintenance of law and order (i.e. the detection of crime and the arrest of offenders); as well as custody of prisoners of war until handed over to detention facilities; surveillance; and control and protection of civilians. Additionally, WW1 was the first conflict where traffic control became an important function. This was identified particularly after the Battle of Loos, when there was huge confusion between two British divisions. During the retreat from Mons in France, the MMPs were busy dealing with soldiers who, through exhaustion or the general confusion of battle, had either lost or became detached from their units. By operating stragglers' posts, the MMPs were able to return soldiers to their units. These posts were also well placed to pick out deserters and those Absent Without Official Leave (AWOL).

The work undertaken by MMPs was not all carried out behind the lines, and sometimes they came under heavy fire. During WW1, the Mounted Military Police suffered 375 casualties. Sixty-five received the Distinguished Conduct Medal and 260 received the Military Medal.

Members of the Corps of Military Mounted Police
taken just before Tom Watts joined them in 1916

DISTINGUISED CONDUCT MEDAL

The Distinguished Conduct Medal (DCM) was established by Royal Warrant on 4th December 1854 by Queen Victoria as a decoration for gallantry in the field by non-commissioned ranks of the British Army. It was the oldest British award for gallantry and ranked only below the Victoria Cross. It was discontinued in 1993 when it was replaced by the Conspicuous Gallantry Cross. Its establishment during the Crimean War states that it was an award to Warrant Officers, Non-Commissioned Officers and men of the British Army for "distinguished, gallant and good conduct in the field".

Prior to its inception, there had been no official medal awarded by the British Crown in recognition of individual acts of gallantry. It was awarded with a gratuity that varied in amount depending on rank. This was given on the recipient's discharge from the Army. Since January 1918 recipients have been entitled to the post-nominal letters DCM.

The medal was struck in silver and is a disk, 36 millimetres (1.4 inches) in diameter. All medals awarded bear the recipient's number, rank, name and unit on the rim. All awards of the DCM were notified in the London Gazette and, during the First World War, details of the citations were generally also included. During the First World War 24,620 DCMs were awarded. This meant that approximately 1 soldier in 350 received this award.

LIZZIE - SYDIE, THE FIRST TO GO

"Sydie was our second son and was always a serious little soul even if he did grow up to have quite a temper if provoked, and he was certainly forceful in his opinions. He did well at school and succeeded in getting into Sir William Perkins School which was very well regarded. I have a lovely school photograph of him, and we were so proud he was doing well.

Young Sydie Watts at Sir William Perkin's School
Second row down third from the left (1899)

Mr. Bailey was headmaster there. Later on he moved to take over as headmaster of the new Stepgates School where Fred went, but more of that later. Mr. Bailey ran a tight ship as they say. He stood no nonsense and the cane was rarely idle but he were fair though. If any lad came home saying he'd had the cane, you could be sure he'd done something to deserve it. Mind you most lads never owned up to having the cane as the chances were they'd get another clout at home for getting the cane in the first place.

Sydie was the first of the lads to join up. He joined the Territorials on 14th September 1914. The date is etched in my mind because it really struck us that this war was going to be very real and affect all of us, not just the regular army and navy. I remember him saying that it was everybody's duty to do something for the war if only to be trained just in case he was needed. All the talk at the time was that it would all be over by Christmas. Anyway as we all know now, it wasn't over by Christmas. Looking back, it had hardly got going. After a family talk around Christmas time, with Tom, Sydie and Albert, it was decided that Tom shouldn't volunteer first because, although he was the oldest, he already his own young family. So Sydie and Albert signed up.

Sydie had been working at Silverlands for some time now and had also been walking out with Ursula, or, as everyone called her, Doll, for quite a while. They had known each other since childhood when William and Adelaide had lived round the corner in St Anne's Road. Their family name was Hall and William was a blacksmith. In fact when Syd and I first married, William used to work at the smithy in Gogmore Lane, just across from Church Walk. William did very well for himself. In the 1890s, the family moved to Sunbury and William set up his own smithy. Sadly that wasn't to last. William died early, not long after our dear Queen. Far, far too early as he was only in his late forties.

Doll and Sydie had been walking out for some years by then and they just seemed so well suited. She was a tall girl, looking Sydie straight in the eye. She certainly had her own mind and could well stand up for herself and her opinions. This was just as well seeing how forceful and, not to say, a bit quick tempered Sydie could be. We hoped that they would marry but the war made such simple things as that so uncertain. We had some lovely photographs taken before the war. They made such a handsome couple.

Sydney Watts and Ursula Hall
Photographs taken about 1910-1912

Sydie joined the regular army at the end of January 1915 and was assigned to the new Army Service Corps that Major Gordon Watney raised in Weybridge. The day after he joined he was promoted to Lance Corporal maybe because of his experience as a fitters mate. We joked that at that rate, another fortnight and he could have been General. Mind you the way the war went on, they'd have been better with men like our Sydie in charge!

He left for the Eastern Mediterranean as part of the Motor Transport Corps. It was hard for all of us, seeing him get on the train. Not just his Father and me, but his brothers and sisters and of course Ursula. We all waved him away, leaning over the edge of the platform vainly trying to catch one last look at the train. Then we all both celebrated and drowned our sorrows in equal measure in the King's Head, before going home to be alone with our thoughts. I was always someone to look on the bright side of things but I somehow couldn't get rid of the thought that the sight of Sydie closing the train door behind him and feeling that him waving might have been the last time I would see him. I couldn't live with such thoughts permanently as I knew in my heart that, while Sydie might have been the first to go, the others might do the same. I just couldn't go on day to day without having hope and believing that we would all be together again.

Sydney Watts with members of 244 Motor Transport Company before embarkation
Sydney is third from the left, middle row

The news Sydie sent home was very restricted and censored, and one time we didn't hear for weeks when he was posted out East. At this time there'd also been no news of the Watney's Boys. But the local press sadly started rumours about how many might have been injured or killed. Though based on what, we never knew. Then one week, in the Surrey Herald, a letter was published from Henry Stanley, who was in the same company as Sydie, reassuring everyone that all was well. I knew of Henry because his father, James, had lived near the Taylors in Victory Road, just off Station Road in Addlestone. James had been a fly driver and Mr Taylor had sometimes used his carriage for trips locally. The letter was a great comfort until we heard from Sydie directly.

'...I am writing these few lines to let you know that the Weybridge lads out here (belonging to the corps which Major Watney raised) are all safe and well at present. We have seen in your paper that rumours have been in circulation concerning some of our deaths, but, up to the present, I am pleased to say, there is not a casualty among us. Immediately your paper arrives we soon gather round the recipient to hear the news of the old village. One paragraph we particularly noticed was that Sergeant Major Yates had written stating that all was well with the Column. I must tell you there are only thirty-five of us out here; they were picked out of the Supply Section. The remainder are 5 days' journey from here, and are no doubt all right. I am pleased to say that everything is going on splendidly out here. We get big shells over occasionally, and we have all managed to dodge them up to the present and I hope we shall continue to do so. There is one thing: our big guns give them all they ask for. Now I must close, with kind regards from all the boys.

I remain, yours obediently,

H STANLEY.'

Extract from letter by Pt. Henry Stanley while serving in Gallipoli
Published in Surrey Herald 16th July 1915

We never knew exactly where Sydie had been out East until he returned and could tell us about it in person. However later we did work out a code to let him tell us a little more about how things were day to day but I'll tell you more about that when we talk about Albert 'cos that's a funny tale to tell.

The first we knew that all was not well was when we got a letter saying that Sydie was being invalided home and would be landing at Southampton. He arrived back in England in January 1916 and was sent straight to the Royal Victoria Hospital just outside Southampton. I went down by train as soon as I could as Syd couldn't get time away from work. The hospital was huge, not just the original brick building, but also the maze of temporary wooden buildings housing the sick and wounded. It took me an age to find where Sydie was - and then the shock of seeing him! Oh, it was heart-breaking. He was so thin and pale. He'd had dysentery, diphtheria and septic poisoning in both legs. The dysentery had cleared up on the voyage home but the state of his legs – he could barely take a few steps. The doctors were careful in what they said but I could tell that they'd been worried about him losing a leg or both. There was little they could do but let nature take its course. I just prayed and prayed when I got home, 'cos it seemed like a miracle was needed.

SOLDIER'S SEVERE ILLNESSES.

A Chertsey soldier who left for the Eastern Mediterranean with the Army Service Corps (Motor Transport) section, raised at Weybridge by Major Gordon Watney, to be subsequently transferred into another Company, has arrived back at Netley Hospital, suffering, and having suffered, from several severe complaints, included in the number being dysentry, diphtheria, and septic poisoning of the arms and legs. The unfortunate fellow is Lo.-Corpl. S. Watts, whose parents live in Grove-road. Watts probably saw as much of the hard struggle in the Eastern Mediterranean as any A.S.C. man, for he was on the Gallipoli Peninsula for several months, and was afterwards despatched to Serbia and Greece before being sent back to Alexandria.

Report of Sydie's return home
Surrey Herald 11th February 1916

When we talked at the hospital, it became clear that he'd had really a hard time. Not long after he arrived out East, he was sent to Gallipoli for several months. We'd read a little bit about the campaign there and how it was going to shorten the war. It sounded like hell on earth and not the great success it was supposed to be. The papers were full of it. Even Churchill, Lord of the Admiralty, resigned. It was a big talking point in the town. No-one expected such a defeat and loss of face, and it felt like a blow to our national pride. Later Sydie always talked with great affection and admiration for the Aussie and New Zealand troops he'd met in Gallipoli. He'd been evacuated with the rest of his company when the campaign failed. They were then moved to Serbia and then Greece where he became very ill with diphtheria and septic poisoning that he put down to frostbite. Soon he was evacuated to Alexandria in Egypt, which he hated, "So hot and all the flies seemed to be everywhere in the hospital, crawling all over you, on everything you ate and everything you touched. But I was one of the lucky ones as the doctors quickly made the decision to send me back to Blighty. Lucky there was a hospital ship ready to go and I got a place on her."

It also came to light that, before he left, Sydie had asked Ursula to marry him whenever he made it back to England. So while he was in hospital, he wrote to his Commanding Officer on 22nd March requesting permission and leave to marry. Happily his CO approved this. I remember his words –

Sir, I beg permission to be married while on Sick Furlough, at present I am at the above address having been invalided from the MEF. Trusting my application will be granted with allowance. I am, Sir, Your obedient servant. Lce Corp Watts

After Sydie's discharge from hospital, they got married on 1st April 1916 at Kensington Parish Church - St Mary Abbots - as this was the nearest church to where Doll was in service at Harmson House. She organised all the banns, the licence, everything. She was so like me – another organised woman who just got on with things! It was just a small affair, like so many war time weddings. So often you heard about sweethearts getting married when a soldier was home on as little as a week's leave and then he was back to the Front. The joy, the worry, the loneliness, the heartbreak and sometimes the sorrow and the grief, you can scarcely imagine it. They were like no other times any of us ever lived through.

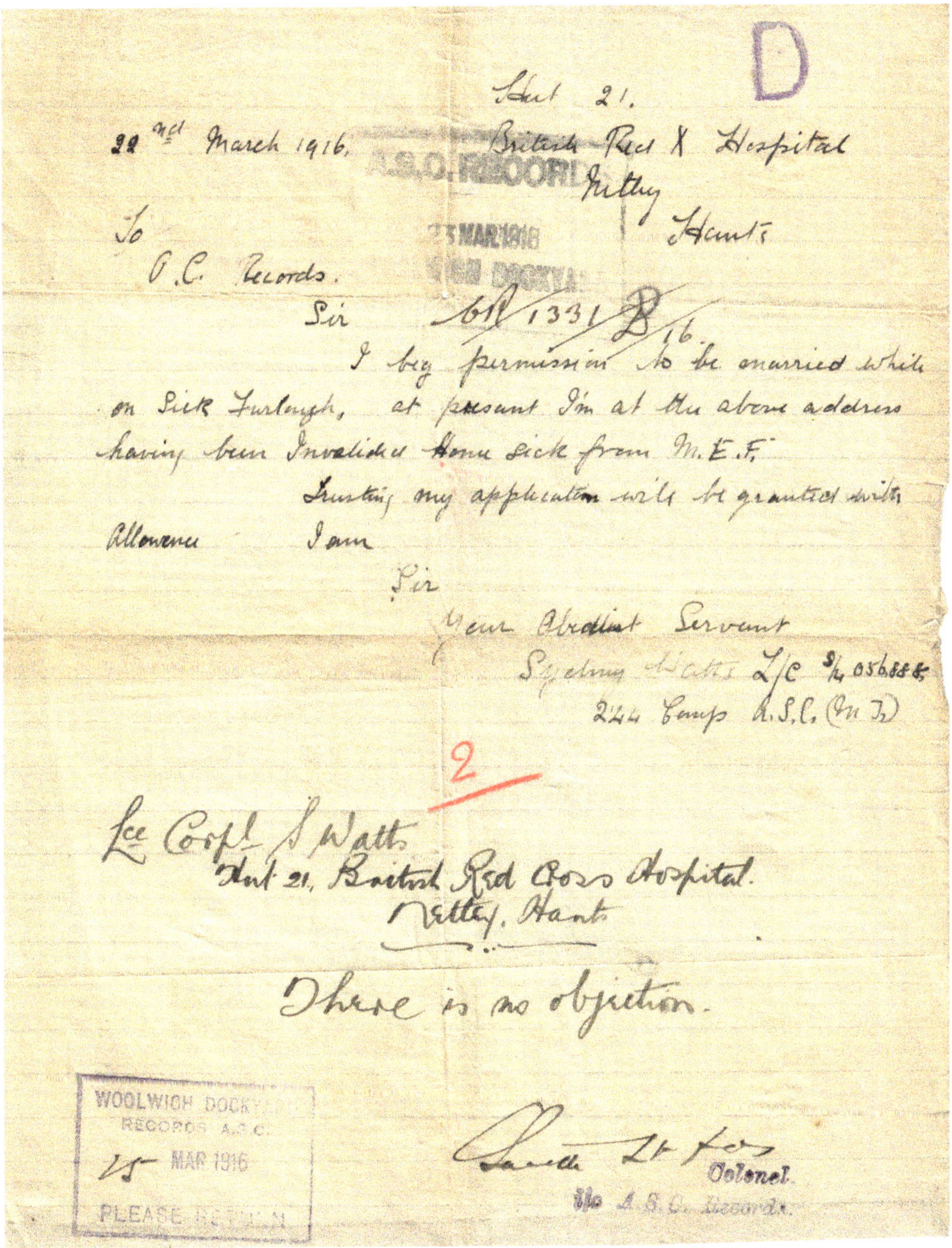

D

Hut 21.
British Red X Hospital
Netley
Hants

22nd March 1916.

A.S.C. RECORDS
23 MAR 1916
WOOLWICH DOCKYARD

To
O.C. Records.

Sir — AR/1331/D/16.

I beg permission to be married while on Sick Furlough, at present I'm at the above address having been Invalided Home sick from M.E.F.

Trusting my application will be granted with Allowance

I am
Sir
Your Obedient Servant
Sydney Watts L/c S/4 056888
224 Comp A.S.C. (M.T.)

2

Lce Corpl S Watts
Hut 21, British Red Cross Hospital.
Netley. Hants

There is no objection.

WOOLWICH DOCKYARD
RECORDS A.S.C.
25 MAR 1916
PLEASE RETURN

[illegible] Lt Col
Colonel.
i/c A.S.C. Records.

Sydney's letter to his CO requesting permission to marry 22nd March 1916

Sydie was still on convalescence leave when they married and they were lucky that a cottage became free down Grove Road, at number 10. They moved in and were very happy while Sydie was still on leave. It was one of the smaller terrace cottages in the road, a bit like our first cottage in Church Walk but with a much longer garden. It had a sturdy Bramley apple tree, just right for pies and crumbles. Unusually, there was also a quince tree and over the years Doll made splendid jelly from this. I'm rambling again; back to the cottage. Just two up and two down but it suited the new couple. Well it wasn't long before we had more happy news, the newlyweds were expecting! A healthy baby boy arrived in the following January, on the 4th, and they called him Sydney too – so that was three Sydneys, all living in Grove Road! So we had my Syd, our Sydie and then young Sonny as his dad liked to call him.

Sydie worked hard getting back his fitness. He went on many a long walk to get the strength back in his legs, often up and around St. Ann's Hill and over the fields to Thorpe Green and back. I daresay he'd an odd pint at the Rose and Crown while he was over there!

Sydney and Ursula on their wedding day, 1st April 1916

When he was assessed as fit, Sydie was called back for duty, not long after the baby was born. Again he was posted out to the East, Mesopotamia this time. We knew little about what was happening out there as most of the news in the papers was about what was happening in France where Tom and Albert were. He sent cards to Doll from Salisbury on his way down to Southampton and then another showing a picture of the ship he was sailing on. He left on 2nd April 1917 on the troopship Cameronia. This was just 1 year and a day after he got married – what an anniversary!

Postcard of HMT Cameronia
April 1917

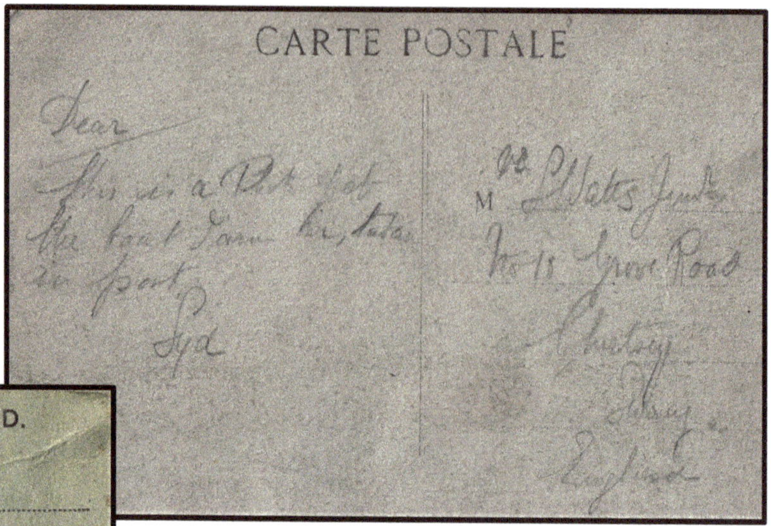

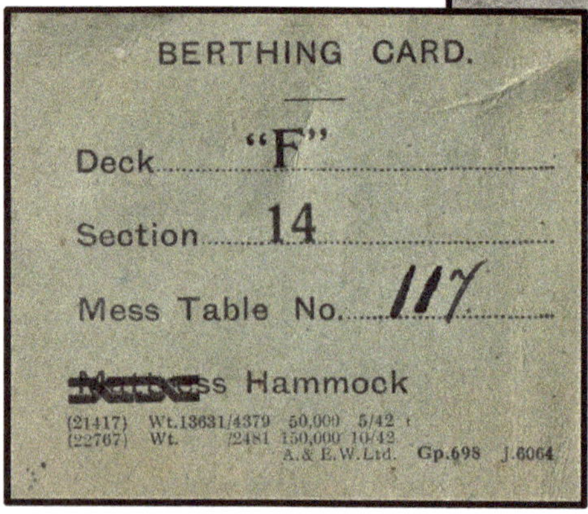
BERTHING CARD.

Deck "F"

Section 14

Mess Table No. 117

~~Mattre~~ss Hammock

(21417) Wt.13631/4379 50,000 5/42
(22767) Wt. 2481 150,000 10/42
A.& E.W.Ltd. Gp.698 J.6064

Postcard notes to home and berthing card details April 1917

It was scarce three weeks later, Sunday lunchtime, when I heard the back door swing back hard on its hinges And Doll burst in clutching little Sydie to her. She was yelling, "Have you heard anything? What do you know?"

"What on earth. Know about what? What is the matter?" I said.

"I've just got this telegram. Have you had anything?"

"No. Let me have a look at it" I took the orange envelope from her hand and pulled out the telegram. All it said was 'Well' and 'Watts'. It was addressed to Mrs Watts at 10 Grove Road. So I said "Let's sit down and work it all out, Doll."

I was thinking aloud, "Obviously something awful has happened and he's needed to tell you that he's alright. That's the most important thing – He's well and he must be safe as otherwise how would he have sent a telegram. What else do we know? Well he's in Malta, it says so at the top."

"But he was on his way to Egypt" said Doll, "How come he's in Malta?"

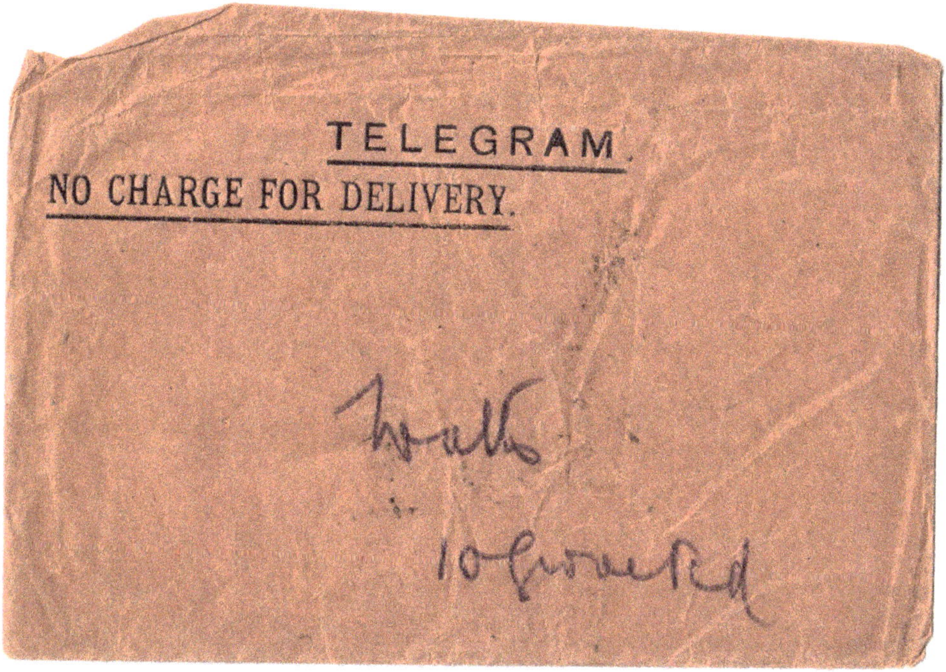

TELEGRAM.

NO CHARGE FOR DELIVERY.

Watts

10 Grove Rd

Telegram to Family Watts, 10 Grove Road
From LCpl Sydney Watts saying he was 'Well'

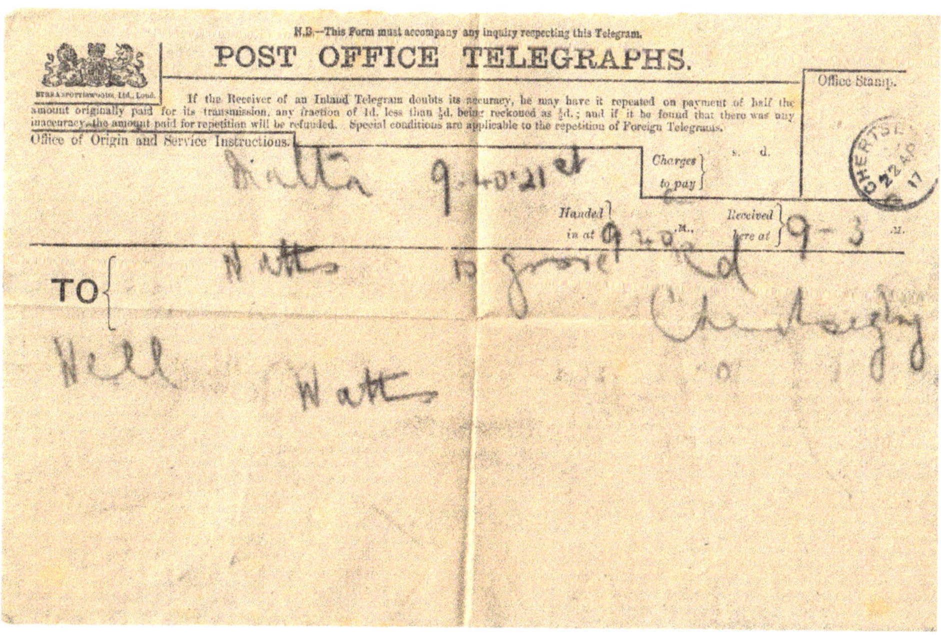

N.B.—This Form must accompany any inquiry respecting this Telegram.

POST OFFICE TELEGRAPHS.

Office Stamp.

If the Receiver of an Inland Telegram doubts its accuracy, he may have it repeated on payment of half the amount originally paid for its transmission, any fraction of 1d. less than ½d. being reckoned as ½d.; and if it be found that there was any inaccuracy, the amount paid for repetition will be refunded. Special conditions are applicable to the repetition of Foreign Telegrams.

Office of Origin and Service Instructions.

Charges to pay s. d.

Handed in at .M. Received here at .M.

TO Watts 10 Grove Rd

Well Watts

"Well Doll, maybe the ship's had engine trouble and had to put in for repairs? No, that won't do, he wouldn't have sent a telegram for that. Maybe he's been invalided off the ship as he's not well? But no, he wouldn't have said he was well would he if that had happened. He'd have said 'Not well but in hospital and recovering' or something like that. So something must have happened to the ship maybe. And there's all those damn U-boats out there. Maybe the ship's been hit and had to put in for repairs. Or the escort ships have been hit and the convoy can't go on without them. Oh I don't know Doll, we're just guessing but at least we know that he's safe. There has to be a way of finding out more. But there's been nothing in the papers that I've seen. What can we do now?"

Syd then joined in and said, "What about this for an idea? It might not work but it could just be worth trying. I'm delivering up at Silverlands tomorrow and if anybody might know a way of finding out more it'll be Sir John, if he's at home. He'll still be in touch with some of his old MPs. I'll talk to Isabella, you know, Miss Dunstan, the Housekeeper. I'll ask her if she can find a way of asking Sir John. I don't know if that's possible but we can only ask. I'm sure he'd like to know as he always held Sydie in high regard when he was working there."

We tried hard to reassure Doll over cups of tea and encouraging her not to worry because at the very least we knew he was well. Needless to say, we spent the afternoon wracking our brains, going round and round and getting nowhere.

Monday passed so slowly until Syd came back from work. Doll had come round and we were there waiting expectantly. As soon as the door opened we chorused, "Well, what happened?"

"Whoa! Let me get in the door first and get my boots off!"

Sitting down in his chair and with a cup of tea in his hand, Syd told us about his visit to Silverlands. "Well, I saw Miss Dunstan and told her what had happened and whether there was any way Sir John could find out more. Well, she could see I was worried and she couldn't have been more helpful. Went straight up to see if Sir John was about in fact. A few minutes later she came back and told me to follow her up into the main house. Well, I've never been there before. Oh, it's magnificent Lizzie. You should see all the paintings and the drapes and the carpets..."

"Leave the damn furnishings out of this and just tell us what happened", I interrupted, maybe a bit brusquely but Doll and me were impatient to know.

"Well, I was shown into the Drawing Room and there was Sir John on his own. He asked me to tell what had happened on my own words. I did so and he simply said 'I can't promise you anything but I will ask some people and see if anything further is known. I liked young Watts, he was a good man with us you know. That's all for now, but I will do my best for you.' He's obviously a man of few words but we've done all we can now and must wait to hear from Sir John."

"Well done Syd, that's all we could have hoped for. You're right; we'll just have to wait now."

Mid-morning Wednesday, there was a knock on the front door. Unusual, as most folk we knew just came straight round the back. I opened it and a man handed me a note saying, "This is from Sir John and he told me to tell you that he hopes you will be relieved. Good day." and with that he left. I rushed inside and opened the note which simply said that the ship, Cameronia, that Sydie had been on, had been torpedoed and sunk but that most men had been rescued. The survivors had been taken to Malta where they were being looked after. So this explained the telegram. Without further ado, I rushed down to number ten and shared the news with Doll.

The next thing we knew was a letter that Doll bought round on the Saturday. Sydie had written giving details of what had happened. In the letter he wrote:

> *'We had a terrible time while it lasted, as we were a whole day's sail from land, so we had about 18 hours on a torpedo boat which was with us; nearly all of us were saved. Of course we lost all else except what we stood upright in and some had hardly anything at all. I must say we all looked proper objects when we landed at Malta*
>
> *We were struck on Sunday, April 15th at about 5.30pm and the boat sunk at 6.15pm so we had time to get pretty well all off, and I must say the men were wonderfully cool. Some jumped straight into the water as soon as it happened, but we waited until all the boats had been lowered and got straight onto the torpedo boat. I can tell you I don't want another time like that – it makes you think of all sorts of things.'*

Another letter came the following day telling Doll that they'd stopped in Marseille and were bound for Alexandria when they were hit by the torpedo. He said there was no warning but everyone had done their duty and stayed calm. He said some men were transferred to the escorting destroyers but some ended up in the water. One thing he did write about was the Captain's Messenger Boy, a little lad with a strong Scottish accent. He'd been on the bridge with the Captain but had a huge megaphone through which he shouted to the troops. 'Keep your heads. There's no hurry. No panic. Everything's going be all right' and so on. He kept on shouting right to the very end refusing to leave until eventually the Captain threw him onto the destroyer which was alongside.

Sydie was safe and well and stationed at All Saints, a convalescent camp near St Georges Bay, somewhere north of Valetta. He said the conditions were good with plenty of food and they were well looked after, plenty of apples – he always loved his apples you know, especially now he'd got the tree in his own back garden.

All Saints' Convalescent Camp, commanded by a New Zealander, was the last stop for convalescent soldiers before returning to the front

Postcard of All Saint's Convalescent Camp St George's Bay Malta 1917

The news even made the local press. Well they were always interested in anything to do with the local lads. I've still got the cutting from the 5th May putting it with all the cuttings I kept that mentioned the lads, including Tom's DCM, Albert's MM and Fred....well I'll come to Fred later.

SOLDIER'S EXPERIENCES.

Pte. Watts, of the A.S.C., whose home is at 10, Grove-road, Chertsey, where his wife resides, has had thrilling experiences in his time. He went through the Dardanelles campaign, and was invalided home in January, 1916. On April 2nd this year he was ordered away again on service. In a letter to his wife, received this week, Pte. Watts (who belonged to Major Gordon Watney's company of the A.S.C. when it was first formed) says the transport he was on board was torpedoed on Sunday, April 18th, and that afterwards it took a torpedo boat 18 hours to land them at Malta. Most of the men saved had nothing but their clothes. The men were wonderfully cool, although some jumped straight into the water at once. They were exceptionally well treated at Malta, where there are plenty of potatoes, green peas and fruit.

Surrey Advertiser 5th May 1917

We were all so relieved that he was safe and well particularly after his ordeals in Gallipoli and the Balkans. We quietly hoped he might be sent home again after this but it was not to be. Our hopes were dashed when he wrote saying he was being sent to Mesopotamia. He ended up in Baghdad, we had to borrow an atlas to find out where that was. Oh, it looked so far from home. He wrote often but the letters sometimes got held up and we'd get several altogether. He even managed to send some photos of him and the other men, some in Arab costume. We'd never seen anything like that before other than on the stage at the music hall. He'd got hold of one of the new cameras, a 'Soldiers Kodak' and said they were very sought after as they were small enough to fit in a waistcoat or tunic pocket. He said his pals all wanted their pictures taken to send home to loved ones, so I think he must have been much in demand.

Left: Sydney in Baghdad
Traditional Arab costume
Below: Seated bottom left
with fellow soldiers.

We never really knew how much action Sydie saw out there until he finally came home and was demobbed on 12th August 1919. We were all so relieved when his journey home from the Middle East passed without incident and all the family gathered at the station to greet him, just like we tried to do for all the others, well except Albert but he always did things his own way."

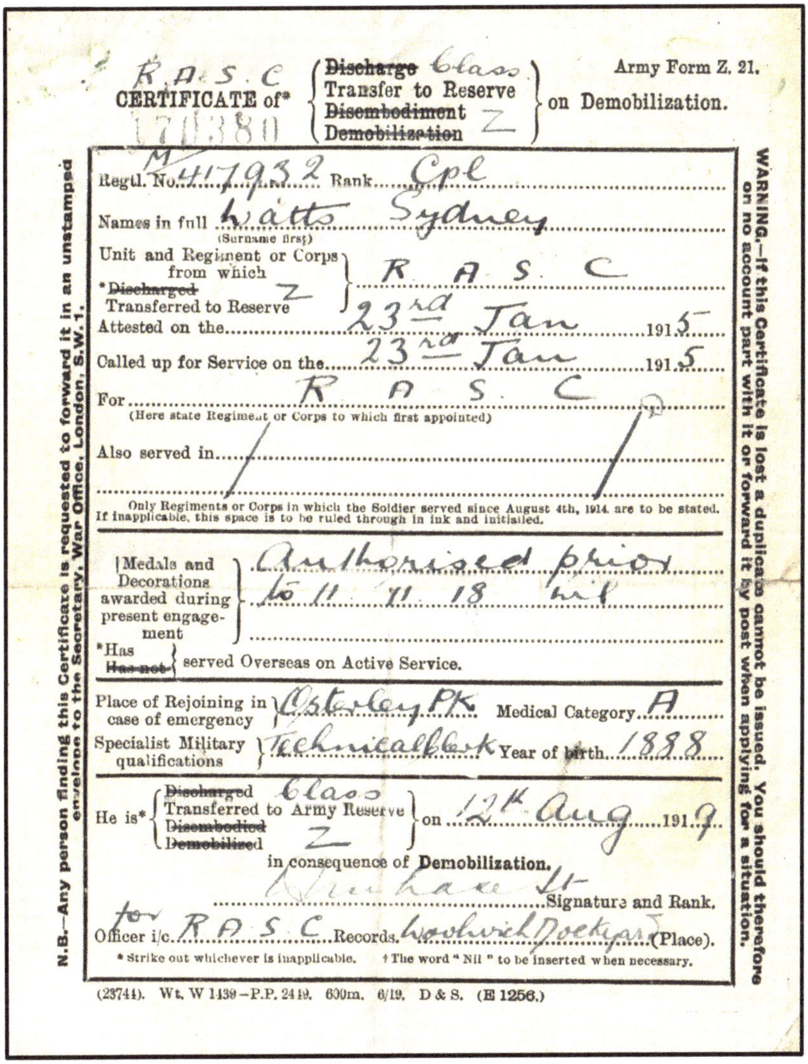

R.A.S.C. CERTIFICATE of* ~~Discharge~~ Class Transfer to Reserve ~~Disembodiment~~ ~~Demobilization~~ Z on Demobilization. Army Form Z. 21.

170380

Regtl. No. M/417932 Rank Cpl

Names in full (Surname first) Watts Sydney

Unit and Regiment or Corps from which *~~Discharged~~ Transferred to Reserve Z: R A S C

Attested on the 23rd Jan 1915

Called up for Service on the 23rd Jan 1915

For (Here state Regiment or Corps to which first appointed) R A S C

Also served in ...

Only Regiments or Corps in which the Soldier served since August 4th, 1914, are to be stated. If inapplicable, this space is to be ruled through in ink and initialled.

†Medals and Decorations awarded during present engagement: Authorised prior to 11 11 18 nil

*Has ~~Has not~~ served Overseas on Active Service.

Place of Rejoining in case of emergency: Osterley Pk. Medical Category A

Specialist Military qualifications: Technical Clerk. Year of birth 1888

He is* ~~Discharged~~ Class Transferred to Army Reserve ~~Disembodied~~ ~~Demobilized~~ Z on 12th Aug 1919 in consequence of Demobilization.

Signature and Rank.

for Officer i/c. R.A.S.C. Records. Woolwich Dockyard (Place).

* Strike out whichever is inapplicable. † The word "Nil" to be inserted when necessary.

N.B.—Any person finding this Certificate is requested to forward it in an unstamped envelope to the Secretary, War Office, London, S.W. 1.

WARNING.—If this Certificate is lost a duplicate cannot be issued. You should therefore on no account part with it or forward it by post when applying for a situation.

(23741). Wt. W 1439–P.P. 2419. 600m. 6/19. D & S. (E 1256.)

Corporal Sydney Watts
Certificate of Demobilization

CAMPAIGNS IN GALLIPOLI, THE BALKANS AND MESOPOTAMIA

When the First World War broke out in July 1914 many believed that it would be over by Christmas that year. However, as 1914 turned into 1915 it was clear that this would not be the case. It was turning into a war of attrition. On the Western Front the fighting had ground to a stalemate but the casualties continued to rise. The politicians and the military commanders in Britain began to look for other ways to attack Germany and to alleviate the pressure on the Eastern Front. The Russian government had asked for a 'show of strength' against Turkey, one of Germany's allies.

Many in Britain, most notably the First Lord of the Admiralty, Winston Churchill, believed that knocking Turkey out of the war would undermine Germany. Also it was considered that attacking Turkey would relieve pressure on Russia, secure the Suez Canal and Britain's oil interests in Mesopotamia. Additionally it was hoped that the action would persuade the undecided Balkan states, including Bulgaria and Greece, to join the Allied side. It was a very temping proposition but it was based on the mistaken belief that Turkey was vulnerable and would be easily overcome.

The plan was to attack Gallipoli, a peninsula in the Dardanelles near the Turkish capital of Constantinople (now Istanbul), and then move inland to capture the capital. The Dardanelles, a narrow 60-mile-long strip of water that divides Europe from Asia, has been of great strategic significance for centuries. It was hoped that once Turkey had been knocked out of the war, the Allies would have access to Russia's Black Sea ports, creating a line of communication to Russia and access to the Russian wheat necessary for Britain's continuing war effort.

In January and February 1915, British and French ships began a naval assault on the Dardanelles. There were heavy losses from Turkish mines in March. Military landings on the Gallipoli Peninsula followed on 25 April. Contained by the Ottoman defenders, a new assault began on 6 August. Each fresh attempt was defeated and the Allies were confined to the Gallipoli Peninsula in appalling circumstances. The campaign lasted until January 1916 and was a costly failure for the Allies, with heavy losses (around 44,000 dead) and no gains made.

A large proportion of the troops in the Allied force were from the Australian and New Zealand Army Corps, better known as ANZACs. More than 11,000 Australians and New Zealanders (over half of all ANZAC troops sent) were killed. Gallipoli has become a key event in the modern history of Australian and New Zealand, giving birth to the ANZAC legend which is still enormously important in those countries today.

By mid-January 1916, all Allied troops had been evacuated and the attack on the Dardanelles abandoned. For Turkey, this was a major achievement. However thousands had died on both sides and total casualties for the campaign numbered more than half a million. For the Allies, the Dardanelles campaign remains one of the First World War's most controversial episodes, with lasting accusations of poor military leadership, faulty tactics including a complete lack of surprise, inexperienced troops, inadequate equipment, and an acute shortage of shells.

There were repercussions at home in Britain as the campaign had given rise to the impression that the Allies were now militarily fallible. Before the evacuation which ended the campaign, Asquith's Liberal administration was replaced by a coalition government. Churchill, the chief advocate of the Gallipoli venture, resigned from the government and then went to command an infantry battalion in France.

In addition to the Gallipoli Campaign, Britain and the Allies were also fighting a separate campaign in the Balkans. Serbia was an ally of Britain, France and Russia. Serbia had successfully resisted the attacks of the Austro-Hungarian Army in the opening months of the War. However, the combined forces of Austria, Germany and Bulgaria overwhelmed the Serbian armies and conquered the country in October 1915. The Serbs retreated through the mountains of Montenegro to Albania, losing over 200,000 men in the winter snow. The survivors were evacuated to the Greek Island of Corfu to regroup.

Lack of resources and political indecision among the Allies had led to delays in dispatching of aid to Serbia until it was too late to help. Eventually a decision was made to land forces at the vital port of Salonika (now Thessaloniki) in the northern Greek region of Macedonia. French forces and British forces began landing at Salonika on 5th October 1915. The British troops, commanded by Lieutenant-General Sir Bryan Mahon with the 10th (Irish) Division and other troops, were exhausted after service at Gallipoli.

The 10th Division eventually went into the mountains around Kosturino in November as the Allies attempted to block the Bulgarian advance. Unfortunately, the troops had not been adequately equipped for a winter campaign in the difficult mountain terrain. By the end of November, more than 1,600 men had been evacuated from the division, with many suffering from frostbite. After a short campaign the Anglo-French forces found themselves back at Salonika. At this point the British advised that the troops be withdrawn. However, the French – with Russian, Italian and Serbian backing – still believed something of strategic importance could be gained in the Balkans. During 1916, further Allied contingents of Serbian, Italian and Russian troops arrived and offensive operations began.

Despite several offensives the front line remained relatively static until 1918, when a major offensive finally resulted in the surrender of Bulgaria on 30 September 1918.

During the Balkan Campaign, malaria proved to be a serious drain on manpower. In total the British forces suffered over 162,000 cases of the disease and over half a million non-battle casualties. Although the campaign seemed to be a low priority for the War Office, the efforts of voluntary medical organisations, such as the Scottish Women's Hospitals and the Voluntary Aid Detachment nurses was invaluable work in supporting the many casualties.

At the outbreak of WW1, the Ottoman Empire, centred on what is now modern day Turkey, was a neutral power. However at the beginning of November, this neutrality was abandoned and the Ottoman Empire declared a military jihad (holy war) against France, Russia and Great Britain, a decision that would prove to have profound effects for the decades to come.

The Ottoman Empire had recently experienced military setbacks in Libya and the Balkans. Its participation in what, up to then had been a European war, was motivated by dreams of new imperial glory and was encouraged by the might of German industrial and military power. The expansion of the war was seen as an opportunity to regain lost territories and incorporate new lands and nationalities into the empire. With Germany as an ally, the Ottoman Empire posed a serious threat to the British Empire, so in a pre-emptive strike, an Anglo-Indian force was landed at Basra. The aim was to protect the Anglo-Persian oil pipeline, which was vital to the British navy.

Very shortly afterwards, the Ottomans launched a surprise attack against Britain's vital supply route - the Suez Canal. The attempt, in February 1915, to break the British defensive line on the Suez Canal failed and resulted in heavy losses for the attackers. At this time, the Allies launched their attack on Gallipoli.

Map of Ottoman and British Empires in the Middle East and NE Africa 1914

The Allies changed the defensive stance at Basra into a risky advance but the Anglo-Indian force was cut off and surrounded about 100 miles south of Baghdad, eventually being forced to surrender. It was proving to be an extremely difficult environment in which to fight. Flies and mosquitoes attacked the troops, many of whom became sick. Malaria was particularly common. Soldiers froze during the winter nights, and were overcome by heat during the summer. Dust turned to mud when the banks of the Tigris overflowed during the rainy season.

London reacted to this setback and the retreat from Gallipoli by reinforcing its efforts in Mesopotamia. A new commander, General Sir Stanley Frederick Maude, assembled a large force of some 150,000 men, equipped with modern weapons. Basra was transformed into a modern port and a centre for transport.

In Egypt also, British forces gained a new commander, General Sir Archibald Murray, and much needed additional resources with the aim of invading Palestine. In order to do so a new water pipe and railway were built across the Sinai desert right to the borders of Palestine. The Palestine campaign had both successes and setbacks, Baghdad was captured but the failure to take Gaza was a key defeat.

The campaigns were also hampered by Germany's resumption of unrestricted U-boat warfare. In the Mediterranean this took a terrible toll on Allied shipping, and this threatened Britain's ability to supply and maintain the war in this region.

The Russian Revolution in March 1917 led to a paralysis of the Russian military effort against both Germany and Turkey, and the mutiny of the French Army meant that even more pressure was put on the British and Commonwealth troops. Britain now faced the frightening prospect of being the mainstay of the war both in Europe and in the Middle East.

The war in Mesopotamia is also well known for the role played by T E Lawrence (known as Lawrence of Arabia), an English officer who was instrumental in supporting the Arab rebellion that played an important part in the eventual success of the Allied campaign.

Significant progress was finally made and General Allenby entered Jerusalem on 11th December, 1917. The Prime Minister, David Lloyd George did not think that victory would be possible in France in 1918 and sought to make Allenby's advance a key focus of Britain's efforts. However, Germany's massive offences on the Western Front during the first half of 1918 forced the government to recall most of Allenby's British soldiers to France. In compensation Allenby did receive replacements from Egypt and a range of other nations of the Empire including the West Indies and Burma (now Myanmar).

In September 1918, Allenby returned to the offensive at the Battle of Megiddo and quickly destroyed the Ottoman/Turkish armies. Damascus fell on 1st October and, on

26th October, Aleppo, the last city to fall in the campaign. Five days later an armistice with the Ottoman Empire came into effect. The war ended with the British occupying the territory that was to become Iraq, Palestine, Trans-Jordan, Syria and Lebanon. Britain's military success had made her the dominant power in the region. The resulting settlement, which led to the creation of much of the current borders of these countries, generated much controversy at the time and has proved to be the source of much of the instability that continues to be seen in the region today.

SINKING OF THE SS CAMERONIA

The troopship which Sydney (Sydie) Watts boarded in 1918 was the SS Cameronia. This was a twin propeller passenger steamship owned by the Glasgow-based Anchor Line, and had been built by D. and W. Henderson and Company at Glasgow in 1911. Before the war the ship provided a transatlantic service from Glasgow to various destinations. She made her maiden voyage 13th September 1911 on the Glasgow - Moville - New York City route. Moville, in Ireland, was a point of embarkation for travellers, especially emigrants, to Canada and the USA. By February 1915, the Cameronia was part of a joint Anchor-Cunard company service on the Glasgow - Liverpool - New York route.

The Cameronia had more than one encounter with a U boat. On 21st June 1915 while sailing into Liverpool, the Cameronia was attacked by a U-boat in the mouth of the Mersey. Captain Kinnaird turned the ship to ram the U-boat which was then forced to dive and break off its attack.

Later in the war, the Cameronia was used as a troopship, and in 1917 set sail from England with troops bound for the conflict in Egypt and Mesopotamia. Having called in at Marseille in France she then set sail for Alexandria in Egypt carrying approximately 2650 troops on board. At that time the Cameronia was commanded by Captain David Bone, a well-known author of sea stories. His best known novel was the Brassbounder, published in 1911 and a copy of which was taken by Earnest Shackleton on his famous expedition the Antarctic in 1914.

The Cameronia was torpedoed on 15th April 1917 by the German U-boat U-33 commanded by Gustav Sieb. The ship sank in 40 minutes, 150 miles east of Malta. Around 200 lives were lost although accounts vary about the exact number. A good number of these died when the first of the Hercules-type flat bottomed lifeboats was launched and capsized. Some of the crew and soldiers were picked up by the escorting destroyers HMS Nemesis and HMS Rifleman. Most survivors had sufficient time to take to lifeboats but because of the threat of the U-Boat they were left to drift overnight. A sloop was sent out from Malta to pick them up the following day. The survivors were taken to Malta with many spending time in All Saints Camp. This was a convalescent camp near St Georges Bay, north of the capital Valetta.

The last man to leave the Cameronia was Captain Bone. After his officers had reported "All clear" and left the ship, the captain jumped from the bridge and managed to catch the stay of the wireless mast on the destroyer alongside – an amazing piece of skill or luck. Later it was reported that his fine seamanship was crucial in saving the great majority of the men on board, as well as the important part played by the courage and the discipline of the crew and troops.

Private William Tindall who, like Sydie Watts, was a member of the Army Service Corps, described his experiences of the sinking in a letter to his father who was a Police Inspector in Wales:

> *"It would be 5.20pm and I and my pal and two more of our draft were at our quarters on the mess table. Two of them were just going to have a shave and my pal and I were just making a cup of chocolate from some ship's chocolate that Tom Hughes gave me in port, when there was a heavy thud, quickly followed by a terrific crash, which for a moment dazed me. However, I quickly regained my senses and was fully alive to what had occurred. I remember seeing nothing but water and wood and various utensils off the tables flying about and I quickly made for the stairs but never reached them.*
>
> *The flood of water, coming through the hole which the torpedo made, knocked me off my feet and fortunately washed me up against an iron ladder in the middle of the hatchway. I knocked the use out of my arm though, striking my funny bone against some object but hung on with my right, eventually climbing up to the top of the ship.*
>
> *I then ran over the deck looking for a lifebelt but failed to find one. Seeing a boat being lowered down the side, I leaped into it. But as we got half-way down it stuck and some silly blighter cut the rope, with the result that we were tipped into the sea. I fell on about 20 chaps and, managing to disentangle myself from the struggle, I struck out.*
>
> *When I had got about 100 yards, I spotted one of the boats and made for that. They picked me up and then we watched the Cameronia go down. We then drifted and rowed about, with the destroyers circling round us and playing the searchlights upon us to keep an eye on us, lest we drifted away one from another. They could not pick us up as they were full up themselves."*

The "Cameronia" sinking by the bow.

Nearly Gone.

Another view of the sinking ship.

The last view of the doomed vessel.

H. M. Transport "Cameronia," which was torpedoed recently.

Boats cotaining rescued people, photographed after the "Cameronia" had disappeared.

The casualties were very slight, thanks to the bravery of the sailors.

Page from magazine showing photographs of the sinking of the SS Cameronia in 1917

The newspapers reported the sinking in some detail and much was made of the bravery of the Captain's Messenger Boy, Mackinnon. He was rescued by one of the escorting destroyers but sadly his story did not have a happy ending. The following year Mackinnon was on the Tuscania which was sunk off the Scottish coast. The story was reported in several newspapers and below is a cutting from the Birmingham Mail.

A WEE GLASGOW HERO.

MACKINNON LOST IN THE SINKING OF THE TUSCANIA.

In the report published of the torpedoing of the Anchor liner Cameronia with troops in the Mediterranean last summer mention was made of the splendid conduct of the captain's boy, Mackinnon. This youngster was on the bridge with the captain when the ship was struck, and he did much to allay the excitement by shouting through the megaphone to the troops, "Keep your heids, men. Dinna get excited. It's a' richt. Nae hurry," and so on. The sight of the small boy with a megaphone as big as himself advising the soldiers to keep cool made many laugh and quieted many nerves. The boy did many other things, and at the end the captain found he had disobeyed orders and was still on the bridge when everyone else had left the ship. When the captain told him to "clear out" he said, "I'll no go till you go, sir." The captain then caught him by the coat and slung him overboard into the destroyer before jumping himself. An eye-witness on the destroyer described seeing the captain and the boy on the bridge of the sinking ship.

The London correspondent of the "Manchester Guardian" hears now that Mackinnon went down in the Tuscania. Probably he behaved there as he did on the Cameronia, and the death he just missed in the Mediterranean came to him off the Scottish coast. In the list of heroes of our mercantile marine there ought to be a place for this gallant wee Glasgow lad.

Birmingham Mail
Wednesday
20th March 1918

U-33 was just one of many German submarines operating in the Mediterranean Sea. The submarine was built as a Type 31 design in Germany and launched on 17th May 1914. At the time of the attack, U-33 was part of the Mittelmeer Flotilla based in Pula, now part of modern day Croatia. During its time in the Mediterranean, it was responsible for sinking 84 ships with a total of 194,131 tons. Its commander at this time, Gustav Sieb, was well known for his other actions in the Mediterranean, most significant being the sinking of the hospital ship RHMS Britannic on 21st November 1916 near the Greek island of Kea, not far from Athens. 30 lives were lost out of a total of 1065 on board. Britannic was a sister ship to the Titanic and was the largest ship sunk in WW1. The Cameronia was the first ship sunk by Gustav Sieb in his new command of U-33, having previously commanded U-73. He was responsible for the sinking of a total of 56 ships during his two U-boat commands. He later served as head of Logistics in the Luftwaffe in WW2 with rank of Generalleutnant. He was arrested by the Soviets in 1945, sentenced to 25 years in prison but was released in 1955 and returned to Hamburg, where he died at the age of 87 years on 14th October 1970.

Kapitänleutnant Gustav Sieb and a Type 31 U-boat. The same design as U-33

U-33 finally surrendered on 16 Jan 1919 and was broken up at Blyth, Northumbria, in 1919-20. At the time Blyth was a centre for shipbuilding where the first aircraft carrier, HMS Ark Royal was built in 1914. It had also been a major submarine base in WW1.

HOW THE CAMERONIA WENT TO HER DOOM.

Destroyers' Wonderful Work in Rescuing Men.

The following narrative was supplied by a survivor to *The Daily Mirror*:—

To Friday and thirteen are usually attributed by popular superstition all manners of evil omens, and I don't know that a very large percentage of our fact-demanding practicalists of the present day are quite free from a lurking tendency to believe against reason that the ill day and number have in themselves some evil quality, some maleficent power. However that may be, here is the fact:—

The Cameronia left on Friday, 13th, with troops aboard and her crew of 240. The weather was warm and pleasant, the sea calm, and the men, because of the absence of mal de mer, in the best of spirits.

It was on the evening of Sunday, April 15, that the Cameronia met her fate. The weather was still beautiful—beautiful from more than our point of view. It was admirable for the purpose of our treacherous water rat foes.

SHIVER THAT CONVULSED SHIP.

I had just finished tea and was in the act of going on deck for a stroll, and to watch the coming sunset. I had just reached the poop, when—bang!—and I knew we had got it.

The explosion was not in itself what might be called tremendous; but the shiver that convulsed the ship had in it the feel of finality. Before the geyser-like torrents of water thrown upwards and aboard by the torpedo had subsided, before the acrid odours of the exploding chemicals had left their nostrils, the crew were at their stations and their duties.

In these first few minutes was the crucial time; and in these first few minutes happened the worst of the disaster. Let me say, and be it remembered, that probably these men and lads, from the Midlands and inland, had never been at sea before.

There was a rush for the boats. The outer boats, the "clinkers," were swung out on booms, ready to be lowered at a moment's notice in such an emergency.

Extract from article in the Daily Mirror 19th May 1917

LIZZIE – MY ALBERT, THE COMIC

"Albert was my fifth child and fourth son, born less than a year after we lost little Henry at such a young age, only 9 months old. So helpless, so sad and nothing we could do to save him. He just wasted away. But now we had brighter things to concentrate on, not that they lessened the pain of losing Henry. Albert was a joy. A happy bouncy baby, always chuckling. He grew up that way too and became the comedian of the family, always seeing something funny in a situation and having us all laughing, even his father. Albert was always close to Fred, his younger brother, sharing the same mischievous sense of humour.

Albert and Younger Brother Fred

Our Albert was not a great one for concentrating in school and he left as soon as he could, probably to the relief of many of his teachers. After a spell as a grocer's assistant, he got a gardening job working up at Foxhills, a grand house just off the road to

Longcross. This suited Albert so much more, he loved being outdoors. It was the home of Lt. General Sir Edward Hutton who'd been at the court of Queen Victoria and was very well known in the area. He was also a customer of Madeley's in town and Syd used to call at the house to collect and check their weekly grocery order with the kitchen staff and the housekeeper.

Albert joined up not long after Sydie and was directed to the Queen's Royal West Surrey Regiment. He didn't see service overseas for a while and spent some of the time in Aldershot with the 11th Battalion. Even when our troops were still in England, the local Women's War Work Group supported them all in preparation for going overseas with shirts, nightshirts, hot water bottles coves and mufflers. Both Albert and Syd got packages from them.

Private Albert Watts 1916
Queen's Royal West Surrey Regiment

Albert was posted to France in May 1916 and I well recall his last home leave before he left as it was the same month that Tom was called up. Tears were shed but we wished them both luck and a safe return and a plea for them to write so we could feel we were in touch.

When Albert wrote he didn't write about the action but as always found funny things that had happened and generally made light of things. He had to be careful what he wrote as all their letters were censored before being posted. We came up with a code for both him and Tom – if they underlined something in the letter, it meant just the opposite. So, "<u>The food is wonderful and always piping hot"</u> meant it were cold and awful. When he came back home on leave near the end of the war, he told us of an occasion with his Lieutenant, who was responsible for censoring the letters that the men sent home, "Sometimes I think you're fighting a different bloody war, Corporal. Trenches are lovely and dry! Hmmm," with a knowing wink. "Yes, Lieutenant, that's right - one without bullets or rats!"

Albert even had the nerve to write to our local Surrey Herald to ask the readers for the gift of a football so they could play when in camp. I've still got the cutting. I heard from Albert later that none other than Dr. Hodgson, who lived at the Cedars near the Herald Office, had him sent a football with a note wishing him good luck!

FOOTBALL WANTED.—Three local soldiers serving in France—Corpl. Ellerby (Addlestone), Corpl. Cranston (Ottershaw) and Pte. A. Watts (Chertsey)—would greatly appreciate the gift of a football, in order to enjoy a game whilst they are in a rest camp. It should be addressed: 40075, Pte. A. Watts, 11th, Queen's R.W. Surrey's, D. Company, 16th Platoon, B.E.F., France.

Football request from Albert published in the Surrey Herald 1916

It was much easier writing to Tom and Albert in France than it ever was for Sydie and Fred. A letter or card usually took less than a week to go either way to France but letters to the East seemed to take forever – weeks and weeks. We, well me mostly, wrote to them every week, just to keep in touch, just to try and keep their spirits up. I used to tell them all sorts of what you might call 'nothing news', just bits and pieces that were happening in the family or in the town. This kind of letter writing became easier over time. At the start it wasn't something we were used to doing but Tom and Albert used to say that they just loved to hear what was happening so that it made them feel as though they still had roots back home and were being remembered. I always tried write to them like I was talking to them in the back room at home over a cup of tea. So before I started, I'd sit down and imagine the conversation in my head, the questions they might ask and what news I had to tell – what was going on in the family, was everybody well, what was happening in the town, what was the gossip, was there any news of other lads who had joined up from Chertsey and so on. I had a set routine, unless something happened that I needed to tell one of them about. I wrote to Tom on Monday, Albert on Tuesday, Sydie on Wednesday and Fred on Thursday. That way I made really sure none of them was forgotten and none got treated any different to the others, just the way I brought them up. Albert, bless him, whatever his playing prankster and joker, when he came back at the end of the war, he'd nearly every letter I ever wrote him in his kitbag. When he showed me, I just burst into tears suddenly realising what they must've meant to him.

But I well remember some of his 'devil may care' attitude changed after the big battle at Messines. Now that made the news in all the newspapers as the big explosion was felt in London. It was only the following week, it was June 1917, that we had a field postcard, just one of those where soldiers had to tick off a choice of message, telling us that he'd been wounded – shot in the shoulder. But Thank God, he was safe and recovering in the field hospital in Dannes Camiers. We then got a postcard from him a week later, apologising for his writing but he was writing with his wrong hand. We later read in the newspapers that the King and Queen had visited Messines – what a shame Albert wasn't still there to greet them!

MISSING AND WOUNDED.

Mr. and Mrs. Muggeridge, of Abbey-road, have received an official intimation that one of their sons—Pte. H. W. Muggeridge, East Surrey Regt. — has been missing since May 8th. Pte. Muggeridge, who was employed by Messrs. Taylor and Bates when he enlisted the month following the declaration of war, did not cross to France until September, 1916. One brother W. Muggeridge, was wounded whilst serving with the R.N.A.S. in the Dardanelles, and another brother, Percy, is with the Devons in India.

Mr. and Mrs. S. Watts, of Grove-road, have learned that one of their sons, Pte. A. Watts, R.W. Surrey Regt., has been admitted to the No. 22 General Hospital, Dannes Camiers, suffering from a gun-shot wound in the shoulder.

THE KING UNDER FIRE AT THE FRONT.

Tour of Messines and Vimy Battlefields.

GREAT AIR ESCORT.

FROM W. BEACH THOMAS.

FRANCE.—Their Majesties the King and Queen have spent twelve crowded days among our soldiers in France.

The King spent most of his days and nights at or near the front.

Twice he was on the battlefield among shells; he visited Messines, Vimy and the Somme; he rode in a Tank; he saw all the newest engines of war; he talked with soldiers of scores of fighting units.

The Queen was chiefly busy among the hospitals and at centres where women work, though she, too, saw something of war.

RISKED THE SHELLS.

During his first full day in France the King fought over again the battle of Messines, patrolled a great part of the field and risked German shells, which fell near enough to make some of the escort nervous for the King's safety.

Surrey Herald
June 1917

Daily Mirror
Monday 16th July 1917

We hoped Albert might get home leave when he'd recovered but when he was fit he was posted straight back to the battalion. The next thing we knew was a postcard from Italy! Apparently they'd been sent down there as reinforcements, but for what? Only four months later, Albert was back in France again near Ypres. Fortunately he did get some home leave this time and was home at the same time as Tom not long after the fire. Albert just turned up without any warning so nobody went to the station to greet him; he just burst through the door yelling 'Guess who's home?' Truth to tell, their homecoming did a little to raise my spirits. At least I'd still got my sons. They'd been away for 20 months without leave, and it had seemed like eternity. Anyway, that was some reunion only saddened by the fact that Albert had to go back to France. But I do remember while he was home he did make us all laugh and lifted our spirits with his very funny imitations of some of the officers in his regiment. He was always a great mimic.

Like everybody else at home, me and his Father, never knew exactly what any of the four lads were doing or what was happening while they were away. Even so, and though we constantly worried, we were so proud of them all, and all that they were doing fighting for us all at home. Then, just after the Armistice had been announced to great joy and relief, we heard that Albert had been right in the thick of things at the end and had been awarded the Military Medal, or the MM as they called it. He'd been part of a raid that involved crossing a big river in a canvas boat. According to the report in the newspaper, which I've still got just like all my other clippings, they took a German Gun Sergeant prisoner and cleared the village, holding it until the rest of their Battalion caught up.

This apparently was the last raid of the Battalion before the Armistice. Albert's account of it even made our local paper. He'd said, 'We had a lot of streams to cross, but everything came off top hole in spite of the pitch darkness'. Albert did tell me a bit more about it when he came home but was always trying to make light of it. Later there was a 'formal announcement' in the London Gazette, so we made sure we got a copy for the family to keep. Just think, my son, in the London press! Mind you, Tom's announcement was only two weeks later in the Gazette on New Year's Eve for his DSM (Distinguished Conduct Medal).

Albert was finally demobilised on 7th February 1919 and it was later that year in September when he was presented with his Military Medal. By then he'd got a job at the Sanatorium at Virginia Water as he couldn't go back to his job at Foxhills, because that had already been filled earlier in the war. I thought at the time that this was probably only temporary and wasn't surprised when he left to join the Metropolitan Police. I think he and Tom had talked about this many times. I was so pleased as it was a good and steady job and also meant he was outdoors for much of the time which had always suited him."

WAR MEDALS FOR CHERTSEY BROTHERS.

M.M. Won in the last Raid.

Following the publication of the names in our issue of Friday, the fact that 55 war decorations had been awarded to men within Chertsey urban district was mentioned by half-a-dozen London papers during the week-end—demonstrating that it was a record of which the district might well be proud, and, compared with population, likely to be equalled by very few districts in England. This fact should assist the Council in its efforts to secure a German gun or other enemy war material.

The list is open for additions, and during the week-end notifications arrived that the D.C.M. and M.M. had been awarded to two Chertsey brothers—Corpl. T. Watts, of the M.M.P., and Pte. Albert Watts, of the Queen's R.W.S. Regt. The wife of the former resides at 34, Windsor Street, and their mother in Grove Road.

Pte. Albert Watts—who has served a couple of years in France, and who prior to enlisting was in the gardens at Fox Hills, the residence of Gen. Sir Ed Hutton—secured his award for gallantry in the field and conspicuous bravery during a raid, in which the Britishers had to cross a swift flowing river, by means of a canvas boat, also for capturing a prisoner, who turned out to be a Machine Gun Sergt. This was the first prisoner captured by the raiding party, who cleared the village and occupied it till the remainder of the Battalion came up. This was the last raid of the Battalion before the Armistice. "We had a lot of small streams to cross, but everything came off top hole, in spite of the pitch black darkness," Pte. Watts has written.

Surrey Herald 1919 Newspaper Report
Corporal Thomas Watts, Distinguished Conduct Medal (DCM)
Private Albert Watts, Military Medal (MM)

Postscript:

In 2018, as part of the events to mark the centenary of the end of the First World War, many Battalion and Regimental War Diaries were released on line. A war diary was a regularly, usually daily, updated formal record required to be kept by military units of their activities. It was therefore possible to find the exact entry in the Queen's Royal West Surreys diary, recording the action in which Albert participated and that led to him being awarded the Military Medal.

The transcript is as follows and a copy of one of the original diary entry pages is shown on page 129.

QUEEN'S ROYAL WEST SURREY REGIMENT WAR DIARY 8TH NOVEMBER 1918

REF MAP SHEET NO 5 TOURNAI

"At 1.30am a patrol visited the point where 'C' Coy (Company) were going to cross the river and observed an enemy working party which was engaged by our artillery. Occasional bursts of artillery fire by the enemy was experienced during the day including a number of gas shells, a direct hit on Bn Hd Qrs **(Battalion Head Quarters)**, by a gas shell, caused six casualties. Two daylight patrols were sent along river bank and were fired on by the enemy. It was decided to try to cross the river again as soon as it was dark enough, and after a conference, a strong patrol under Capt. HEDLEY MC was ordered to cross the river at the M in MEERSCHE and reconnoitre the village, if no opposition was met, the village to be occupied and patrols pushed out, if opposition was met with, to secure identification and withdraw. At this period there were not any indications of an enemy withdrawal. A collapsible canvas boat was procured and a section of Royal Engineers under Lt SHAW RE, took charge of the operation of getting the patrol across the river. The situation was fairly quiet with the exception of occasional bursts of MG **(Machine Gun)** fire, the boat was launched, and, at 9.00pm the crossing commenced, the boat was first paddled across by means of shovels, this proved to be very difficult on account of a very strong current running at the time, but it was accomplished and a rope was secured to either end of the boat in order to pull it backwards and forwards. The crossing of the patrol was completed in five journeys as the boat would only hold 8 men at a *time, and the patrol pushed on to the village. At this period very close touch was kept with the French on the left who were attacking at 5.50am on the 9th.*

At 11pm a message was received from Capt HEDLEY to the effect that he had cleared the village of the enemy. Orders were immediately issued for the remainder of the Battalion to cross the SCHELDT. 'C' Coy at KERKHOVE was at this time endeavouring to cross the river at GRIJKOORT but the enemy was very active there, and it was given up. The whole battalion crossed the river by means of the one boat. (Casualties Nil)

9TH NOVEMBER 1918

At 12.01am an order was issued to OC (Officer Commanding) 'D' Coy (Capt HEDLEY) to push on and make good the AUDENARDE – BERCHAM Railway, at 1.30am a message was received from the French Commander to the effect that they were assisting in the operation. At 3am the whole of the battalion had crossed the river and was established in MEERSCHE. 'C' Coy was ordered to push out on the right, and send patrols in the direction of BERCHEM, this was done, the patrols entering BERCHEM and capturing a prisoner."

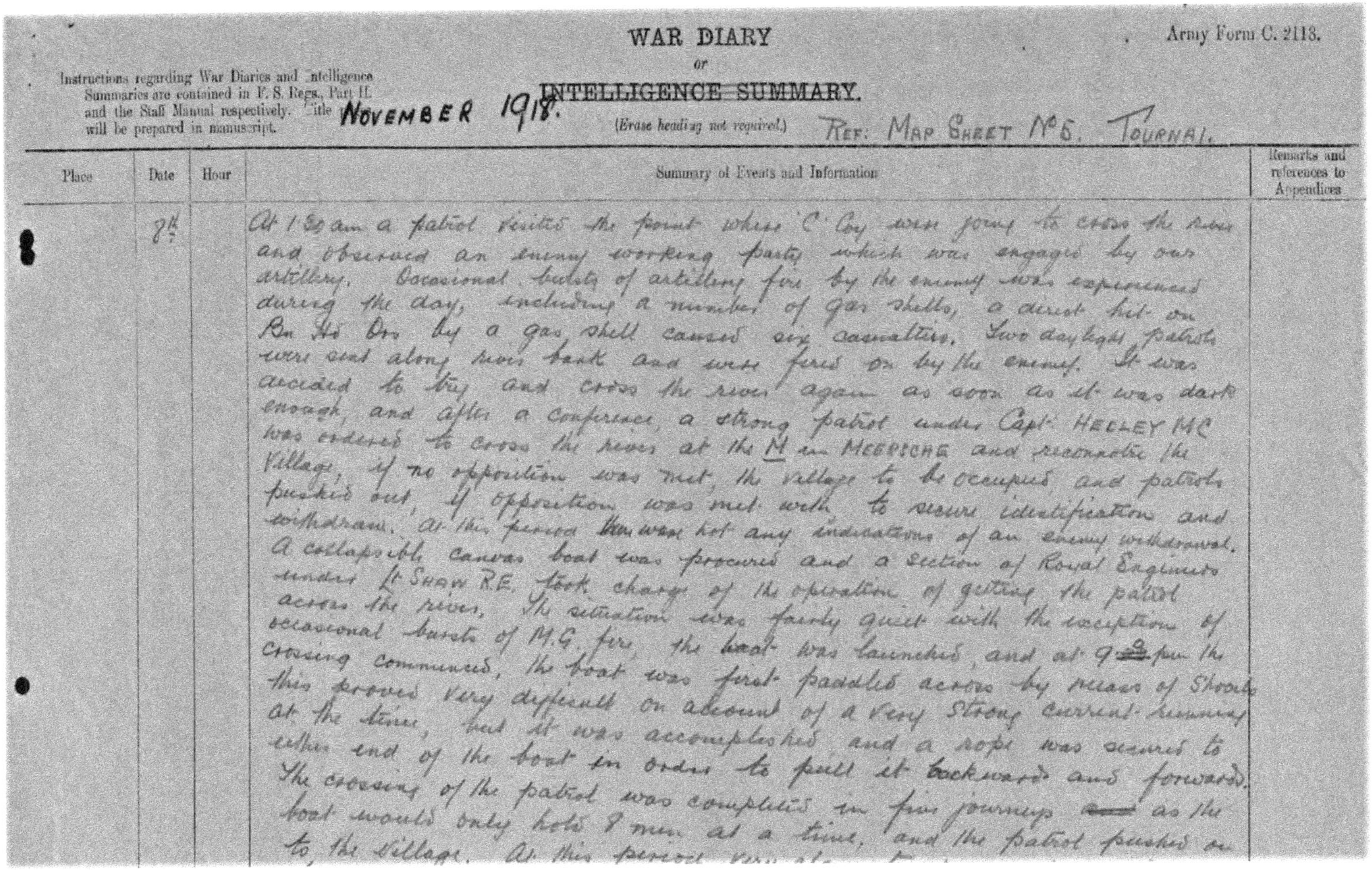

WAR DIARY
or
~~INTELLIGENCE SUMMARY.~~
(Erase heading not required.)

Army Form C. 2118.

Instructions regarding War Diaries and Intelligence Summaries are contained in F. S. Regs., Part II. and the Staff Manual respectively. Title pages will be prepared in manuscript.

NOVEMBER 1918. REF: MAP SHEET No 5. TOURNAI.

Place	Date	Hour	Summary of Events and Information	Remarks and references to Appendices
	8th		At 1.30 am a patrol visited the point where 'C' Coy were going to cross the river and observed an enemy working party which was engaged by our artillery. Occasional bursts of artillery fire by the enemy was experienced during the day, including a number of gas shells, a direct hit on Bn Hd Qrs by a gas shell caused six casualties. Two daylight patrols were sent along river bank and were fired on by the enemy. It was decided to try and cross the river again as soon as it was dark enough, and after a conference, a strong patrol under Capt. HEDLEY MC was ordered to cross the river at the M in MEERSCHE and reconnoitre the village, if no opposition was met, the village to be occupied and patrols pushed out, if opposition was met with to secure identification and withdraw. At this period there were not any indications of an enemy withdrawal. A collapsible canvas boat was procured and a section of Royal Engineers under Lt SHAW R.E. took charge of the operation of getting the patrol across the river. The situation was fairly quiet with the exception of occasional bursts of M.G. fire, the boat was launched, and at 9[illegible] pm the crossing commenced, the boat was first paddled across by means of shovels, this proved very difficult on account of a very strong current running at the time, but it was accomplished and a rope was secured to either end of the boat in order to pull it backwards and forwards. The crossing of the patrol was completed in five journeys as the boat would only hold 8 men at a time, and the patrol pushed on to the village. At this period [illegible]	

Photographic Copy of Original War Diary Entry
Queen's Royal West Surrey Regiment
Three days before the Armistice
8th/9th November 1918

It has also been possible to confirm the weather conditions for this raid from the Meteorological Office Daily Records of the time. There was rain overnight giving way to an overcast sky with a gentle northerly breeze and less than a quarter crescent of the moon - perfect cover for a raid. One of the Met Office charts for that Saturday morning is shown below.

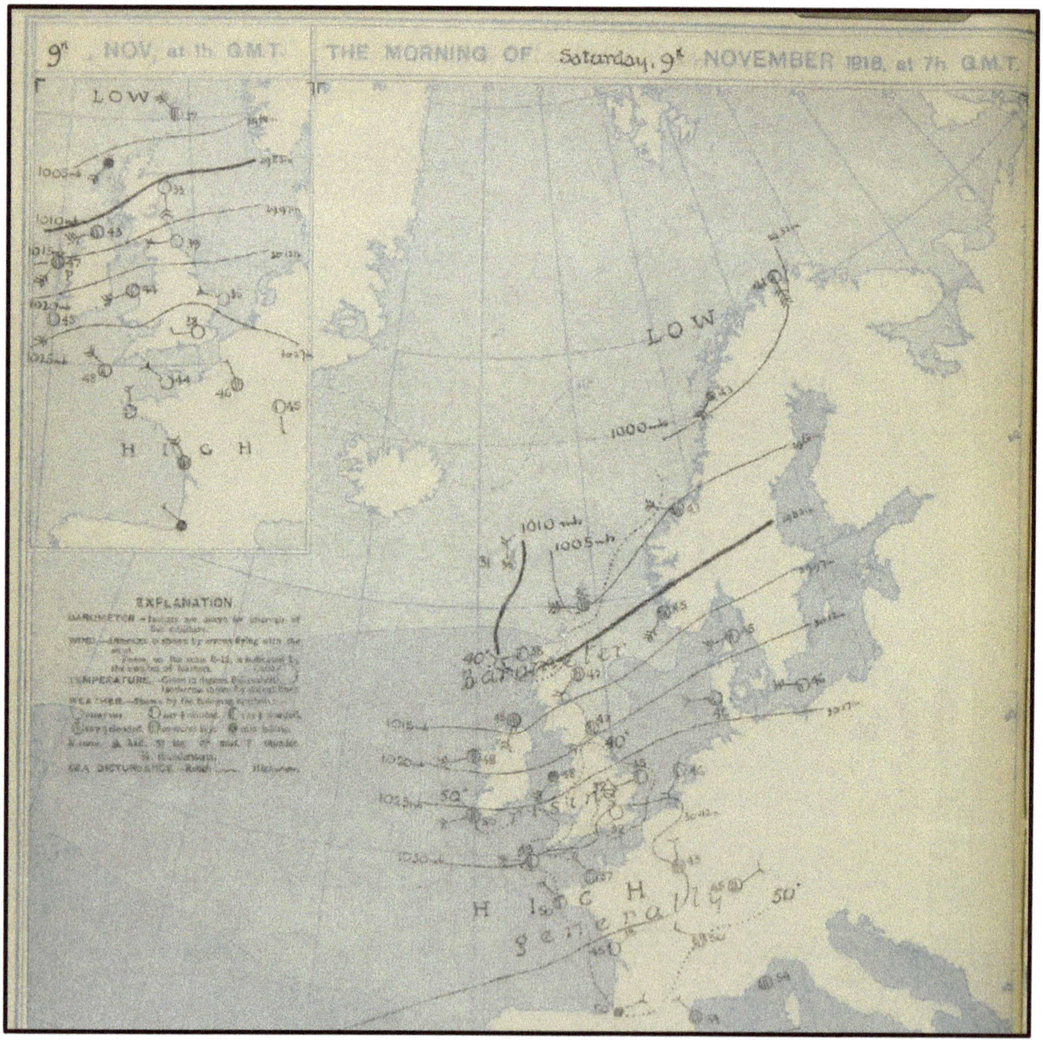

Reproduced with kind permission of Her Majesty's Government.
"Contains public sector information licensed under the Open Government Licence v3.0"

MAIL SERVICE

During the Great War, as in wars before and since, the efficient and effective delivery of mail was crucial to the well-being and morale of soldiers at the front and also civilians at home. Soldiers saw it as a vital reassurance that those at home remembered and loved them and that their welfare mattered to them. Letters were eagerly awaited and acquired a significance that should not be underestimated. However letters and postcards were not the only evidence that a soldier remained central to his family and his community. Parcels, too, provided material and psychological comfort particularly when faced with an inadequate diet and uniforms that provided poor protection from the harsh conditions found in the trenches. Home-made cakes, jam and suchlike gave pleasure, variety and essential nourishment. Warm clothing including socks, scarves, gloves and blankets kept out the worst of the elements. Information in the form of local newspapers kept soldiers in touch with their communities; and mementos such as photographs or a lock of a sweetheart's or baby's hair became cherished objects.

Basil Clarke, a journalist, writing in *The War Illustrated*, said "Letters from home were as essential in their way to a soldier in the field as food and supplies; for just as food is needed to keep him in fighting trim, so is news of relatives and friends to keep him in good spirits and fighting mood."

Similarly, families at home depended upon the regular delivery of mail for continued reassurance that their loved ones remained, at least for the moment, unharmed. When lapses in correspondence inevitably occurred, for a variety of reasons, families waited at home with understandable and mounting anxiety, eager for news whilst trying to avoid reading too much into newspaper reports from the Front.

Well before the War, in February 1913, the War Office had authorized the formation of a military postal unit - The Royal Engineers, - Special Reserve, Postal Section. (R.E.P.S.). The staff for this new unit were recruited solely from post office personnel. At the outbreak of War, the R.E.P.S. had a staff of 300, which was thought to be sufficient to serve an expeditionary force of six divisions and a small Army Postal Depot in London. The overseas contingent was intended to provide Field Post Offices (FPOs) for the serving army. It was quickly apparent that this would be woefully inadequate given the expansion of the army planned by Lord Kitchener.

Initially, an ordinary letter service and a parcel service were provided, and also F.P.O.s sold stamps and dealt with postal orders and telegrams. At the start of the War, letters and parcels destined for the B.E.F (British Expeditionary Force) went first to the Home Depot (H.D.) that had been established at Mount Pleasant, London which was staffed by 30 men of the R.E.P.S. Within weeks, as the volume of mail grew, both the Army Parcels Office and the Army Letter Office moved to much larger new premises capable of dispatching 2,000 bags of mail a day to the B.E.F. The demand continued to grow and in May 1915, the number of staff at the Home Depot increased to five officers and 563 other ranks. From that point on, as more workers were needed, women civilians and disabled soldiers were then taken on. At the height of the war well over 2,800 soldiers and civilians were employed at the Home Depot, which moved to a specially constructed timber building covering five acres in Regent's Park.

R.E.P.S. Post Office Sorting, Regents Park Home Depot, London

The relative closeness of the battle fronts to home – London to Ypres was less than 140 miles as the crow flies – made it possible for families to stay in regular contact with soldiers at the Front. It was possible for a letter mailed in London to arrive at the Front in three days. However it would take longer from other parts of Britain. Parcels sent from England to France usually arrived at the Western Front within a week. Return mail home usually took longer, mainly because letters had to be read and censored by an officer to ensure that no sensitive information was being sent. Also, embargoes were usually placed on all outgoing mail prior to any major offensive. The extensive railway networks in both Northern France and Britain were an essential component in this very efficient and speedy service.

By 1917, British soldiers were sending home between 1 and 2 million letters and postcards every day. Writing about the Home Depot in 1917, Basil Clarke said, "No fewer than twelve million letters a week and not short of a million parcels ... were sent to this office from all parts of the country, all letters bearing the magic words B.E.F. Every post office of any size has its special B.E.F. bag or bags for London, and all hours of the day and night trains are arriving in London with their loads of B.E.F. bags for our soldiers in the field in France."

Predictably, demand on the system was highest at Christmas and New Year and can be seen in the photograph below taken in December 1917.

Letters home were free of postage. But those sent from Britain did incur postage, the costs of which, particularly for parcels, could be an onerous expense especially for poorer families.

Although subject to censorship, soldiers used the correspondence to confide their anxieties, their hopes for the future, their love and affection for their sweethearts, wives, children and parents. They sent home sentimental souvenirs as well as asking for clean socks, warm gloves, palatable food and many other necessities plus occasional luxuries as Albert Watts did, asking for a football.

In return, loved ones and families wrote telling of everyday life in an effort to stay connected and sent parcels on a regular basis. Often parcels would be sent from women's groups who knitted and sewed items for the soldiers. Most towns across the country had such a group including Chertsey.

Overall, the nature, extent and frequency of the communication speak volumes about how combatants remained connected psychologically and emotionally to the families they had left at home. The generation of 1914 grew up in an age of widespread but not yet universal literacy. British children were introduced to the art of letter-writing in the elementary curriculum of the time. Many more would have made use of the ubiquitous penny postcards which had become so popular in the years before the War. From the 1890s onwards, when discounted postage rates for cards were first introduced, the affordable and all-purpose illustrated postcard became the preferred way for working people to stay in touch. The frequency of the postal service was such that postcards posted one evening would be received the following morning and the reply received the same evening. At that time, the postcard was often referred to as the "poor man's telephone."

Postcards from the Front took many forms from the standard army field service postcard to the silk embroidered cards made by local women and sold to the soldiers.

Postcard publishers actively encouraged soldiers to write home to family and friends and even urged children to send a letter to their soldier fathers and brothers. Central in these illustrations was the iconic red pillar-box.

Right from the start of the War, the Army Postal Service realized it had problems regarding censorship. One way of tackling this was by supplying soldiers with a Field Service Postcard, known as 'Army Form A2042'. On the address side it carried an imprint of a penny stamp, and on the back it had a series of messages which could either be 'retained' or 'deleted'. In this way essential information was conveyed to the recipient about the sender's well-being without the need for the card to be censored. The soldier was not allowed to write anything on the Field Service Postcard except his name and the date. In addition the soldier was warned: "**If anything else is added the postcard will be destroyed.**"

All other mail was read and censored by an officer which led to other comic postcards being printed to satirise this.

Soldiers and families often sought to find creative ways around censorship, or simply express their feelings in a more private way. Even the position or orientation of the stamp on a postcard could be used as a code.

It cannot be overstated how important the transmission of mail was to the morale and well-being of both serving soldiers and those they had left behind. It was a huge operation which, for the most part, ran smoothly and efficiently and was highly valued by everyone.

MILITARY MEDAL

The **Military Medal** (**MM**) was a military decoration established on 25 March 1916 and awarded to personnel of the British Army and other arms of the armed forces, below commissioned rank, for “acts of gallantry and devotion to duty under fire." The award was discontinued in 1993 when it was replaced by the Military Cross. It ranked below the Distinguished Conduct Medal (DCM) but awards were announced in the London Gazette. The MM attracted a gratuity and the recipient was allowed to use the letters MM after their name. During WW1 nearly 116,000 MMs were awarded. This means that approximately 1 soldier in 75 received this award.

LIZZIE – FRED, MY YOUNGEST TO SERVE

"Now Fred was my youngest to serve in the Great War. He was the last to join up but he'd certainly tried hard for that not to be the case....I'll come onto that.

He was one of the first children to go to the new Stepgates School that was built in the town. It was a wonderful new school opposite the playing fields that Mr Tulk would later donate to the town. Fred did well enough in his lessons but maybe there was just a bit too much of Albert's influence working I always thought. I still have the picture of him in his class group at the new school.

Fred Watts with his class group.
Fred is first row down from the top third from the left.
The caption board reads:
CHERTSEY STEPGATES COUNCIL BOYS SCHOOL SEPTEMBER 1908 STANDARD 11

The new Stepgates School opened in 1908
It was a huge leap forward for education provision in the town
Separate schools for boys and girls

When he left school he got a job nearby in town. Then, out of the blue, one Saturday he came back from town and proudly announced, 'That's it! I've signed on and I'm joining Tom and Albert and going to France!' Well, you could have heard a pin drop. It were 1915 and he were only 16 years old. 'I've been to the Town Hall and seen the recruiting Sergeant. I've got my paper here' he said proudly waving it above his head.

I'd never seen his father so angry. His face went red and he yelled, 'You'll do no such bloody thing. Give me that!' grabbing the paper out of Fred's hand. 'Right, give me my coat Lizzie'. Turning to Fred and telling him in no uncertain terms, "We're going out. Right now – with me!" With one movement he had his coat on and had Fred by the scruff of his jacket, and they were out the back door with Fred protesting all the way up the passage way and onto the street. I'm I could still hear him as they turned the corner into Alwyns Lane.

Half an hour or so later they returned with Fred red-eyed. I think he'd been crying at some stage and Syd looking both cross and relieved. "We saw the recruiting Sergeant and I told him the lad's only 16 so he can't sign on. Will you take his name off the list?"

Well apparently there were much toing and froing but it were finally agreed, and Fred was crossed off the list and his papers torn up. Trouble was, at that time, you didn't need to give proof of your age or even the right name, as we heard about some lads, in order to join up. They were so desperate for volunteers. "'You can think about it and when you're 18, same as the others, you can make your own mind up then and not before. Right. There, that's all said now", which was always Syd's way of shutting down any discussion and signalling that the matter wasn't to be talked about again. The decision was final.

Well, Fred clearly wasn't happy but there was nothing he could do. The next day, I had a long heart to heart with him before Syd got back from work. I hoped I'd explained why his father had been so angry and just why he should wait until he was of age. No-one would think any the less of him that he was too young to enlist then. Anyway, as soon as he was 18, his mind was well set and he joined up for real. He was sent to the King's Royal Rifles for training. Saying goodbye to Fred was the hardest of all. At the start of the war I never expected that it would last long enough for him to be caught up in the fighting. I'd always hoped that at least he would be safe. Because of that, I found it so hard to let him go. He was sent to France, promoted to Lance Corporal and promptly got wounded, just like Albert.

Private Albert Watts Queen's Royal West Surrey Regiment
Lance Corporal Fred Watts King's Royal Rifles

After Fred recovered he was posted to Egypt at the end of 1917 only to follow in one of his brother's footsteps again – his ship, the Aragon, was torpedoed on its way from Malta. It made our local papers again in January 1918. We just couldn't believe that lightning would strike twice with both of them being torpedoed.

BROTHERS ON TORPEDOED SHIPS. — Mr and Mrs. S. Watts, of Grove-road, have learned that their youngest son, Lce.-Corpl. F. Watts, was on a ship recently torpedoed near Malta, and was rescued after spending a lengthy period afloat in a small boat. Many readers will recollect that Mr. and Mrs. Watts' second son, Pte. S. Watts, of the A.S.C., was also on a boat torpedoed near Malta. Four brothers of the family are now serving in four distinct phases of the world-war—France, Italy, Egypt and Mesopotamia.

Newspaper report of Fred's rescue from torpedoed ship
Surrey Herald 18th January 1918

Again we didn't know anything about the sinking of the Aragon until he was safe. We heard that he'd been sunk after the ship left Malta but that he was safe. It wasn't until later when we got a letter from Fred that we knew he'd been near Egypt and had been rescued to Alexandria. It became a lot clearer when the official news was released and there were reports in the national papers and our own local papers.

When he got home at the end of the war he told us bits about the terrible time of the U-boat attack when two ships went down within the hour. I always felt he was keeping a lot of detail back or just didn't want to talk about it. Fortunately, Fred was one of the 'lucky ones' who'd managed to jump from the troop ship and was picked up by a small boat. He said there were many soldiers who were 'rescued' onto the destroyer only for that to be torpedoed and sunk in less than an hour.

Fred just didn't seem to have any good luck. While he was out there in the East, he caught malaria and spent some of his posting in hospital. Maybe his luck did change, when he was sent back home at the end of 1918 he was the first of the lads to be demobbed in January 1919. At last I had one of them home safe and sound."

WW1 RECRUITMENT

The expansion of the British Army from the small professional force of 1914 to a huge citizens' army, capable of defeating the German and Austro-Hungarian armies was a massive exercise in recruitment, training and deployment.

At the start of World War I, the British Army consisted of eleven divisions of which four were stationed in India and were not immediately available for service in Europe. Fourteen Territorial Force divisions also existed, and 300,000 soldiers in the Reserve Army. Lord Kitchener, the Secretary of State for War, considered the Territorial Force inadequately trained for immediate deployment. Furthermore he thought that the regular army should not be wasted in immediate battle, but used to help train a new army with a minimum of 70 divisions that he foresaw would be needed to fight a lengthy war. This would match the size of the French and German armies.

By the end of the First World War almost 1 in 4 of the total male population of the United Kingdom of Great Britain and Ireland had joined up, over five million men. Of these men, 2.67 million joined as Volunteers and 2.77 million as conscripts.

For more than a century, British government policy and public opinion was against conscription. The forces, both Army and Navy, had been manned by voluntary recruitment. Since 1908 the British Army had offered four forms of recruitment. A man could join the army as a professional soldier in the *Regular Army* or as a part-time member of the *Territorial Force* or as a soldier of the *Special Reserve*. Finally there was the opportunity to join the *National Reserve*.

On his appointment as Secretary of State for War shortly after war was declared, Field-Marshal Lord Kitchener called for volunteers to dramatically increase the size of the army. The public response to this was amazing with almost half a million men enlisting in two months

At the outbreak of war the population of the parish of Chertsey (including Addlestone) was around 14,000. Within a week of the declaration of war over 500 men from Chertsey and Addlestone had volunteered, most registering at the Chertsey Recruiting Station in the Town Hall.

At one point the 500 all congregated on the Recreation Ground on Guildford Road, next to Sir William Perkins School, awaiting their instructions. Even the local sport was affected as Chertsey Football Club suspended all matches to help stimulate recruitment. The Surrey Herald reported on 23rd October 1914 that members of the 6th East Surrey Regiment had set off from Chertsey Station to the accompaniment of 'It's a Long Way to Tipperary' played by the band of the School of Handicrafts. They were given gifts of cigarettes, fruit and books for their journey. Nationally this initial enthusiasm soon died down to average around 100,000 men per month. This was not sufficient for Kitchener's needs so plans had to be made to encourage further enlistment.

Your King & Country Need You.

A CALL TO ARMS.

RECRUITS WANTED IMMEDIATELY

FOR THE

REGULAR ARMY.

EXTENSION OF AGE LIMIT.

Between the ages of 19 and 35 years; Ex-Soldiers up to 45, and certain selected Ex-Non-Commissioned Officers up to 50.

Men desirous of serving their Country should attend at any of the following addresses:

THE BARRACKS, KINGSTON-ON-THAMES.
THE TOWN HALL, KINGSTON-ON-THAMES.
(5 to 8 each evening).
24, HILL STREEET, RICHMOND.
6, BEAMISH ROAD, PUTNEY.
467, YORK ROAD, WANDSWORTH.
186, LORDSHIP LANE, EAST DULWICH.
151, HIGH STREET, TOOTING.

COUNCIL CHAMBERS, MERTON.
VESTRY HALL, MITCHAM.
THE THEATRE, WIMBLEDON.
DRILL HALL, SUTTON.
3, HOOK ROAD, EPSOM.
MUNICIPAL BUILDINGS, LEATHERHEAD.
CONSTITUTIONAL CLUB, WEYBRIDGE.
TOWN HALL, CHERTSEY.
LITERARY INSTITUTE, EGHAM.

GOD SAVE THE KING.

Notice placed in the local Surrey Herald & Surrey Advertiser

Regular Army

It was still possible to enlist into the regular army on standard terms which was usually for a term of twelve years – 7 years active and 5 years on reserve. However, Lord Kitchener's issued instructions in August 1914 for a new form of "short service" under which a man could serve for "three years or the duration of the war, whichever the longer". Men joining on this basis, including all of "Kitchener's Army" and the "Pals" units were technically full members of the regular army.

The wartime volunteers continued to have some choice over the regiment they joined and they had to meet the same physical criteria as the peace time regulars. They had to be taller than 5 feet 3 inches and aged between 18 and 38. However, recruits were not sent overseas until aged 19. However there are many recorded instances of underage and indeed overage men being accepted into the service. It was not necessary to produce evidence of age or even of one's name in order to enlist. This was the 'loophole' that Fred Watts sought to exploit by trying to join up when he was underage. It is estimated as many as 250,000 underage boys may have volunteered; either by lying about their age or giving false names which recruiters often turned a blind eye to.

The famous 'Kitchener' recruitment poster seen all over the country

Territorial Force

Enlistment into the Territorial Force remained open, and it was mobilised in August 1914 when its men were then viewed as being full-time service. Men joining from September 1914, like Sydney Watts, were expected to sign the "Imperial Service Obligation", which gave the army powers to send them overseas or to transfer them to a different unit if required.

One interesting development was the formation of 'Pals battalions'. These were groups of men from the same town, factory, football team or similar groups joining and fighting together. Lord Derby first made the suggestion at a public meeting, and within three days, he had enough volunteers for three battalions. Lord Kitchener immediately gave official approval for the measure and the response was staggering. Manchester alone raised nine specific Pals Battalions. One of the smallest towns was Accrington, in Lancashire, which raised one battalion. Sadly one consequence of Pals Battalions was that a whole town could lose its military-aged menfolk in a single battle as tragically happened to the 'Accrington Pals', who went 'over the top' on day 1 of the Battle of the Somme. Shockingly, 584 of the 720 troops were killed, wounded or missing.

Bradford & Keighley example of recruitment notice for PALS regiments

Sydney (Sydie) Watts joined the Pals Company raised by Major Watney of Weybridge, which became part of the Army Service Corps as 244 Motor Transport section. Albert Watts joined up for the 'short service' option shortly after Sydney.

On 11th October 1915, Lord Derby, who had played a major part in raising volunteers, was appointed Director-General of Recruiting. He brought forward a scheme five days later, often called the Derby Scheme, aimed at increasing the numbers of recruits. Each eligible man aged 18 to 41, who was not in a "starred" (essential) occupation, had to make a public declaration through a process known as 'attestation'. The process was complex and a huge undertaking. Each eligible man's blue card from the recently completed National Register was copied onto a pink card. This was in turn sent to his local constituency's Parliamentary Recruiting Committee. The Committees had appointed canvassers who were "tactful and influential men" not liable for service. Apparently discharged veterans and fathers of serving men proved very effective.

Each eligible man was also handed a letter from Derby explaining the programme, emphasizing that they were in "... a country fighting, as ours is, for its very existence ..." Face to face with the canvasser each man had to declare whether or not he would attest to join the forces. This had to be done individually and no one was permitted to speak for him. Those who answered positively promised to go to the recruiting office within 48 hours. Many were often accompanied there immediately. If found fit they were sworn in and paid a signing bonus of 2 shillings and 9 pence. The following day they were transferred to Army Reserve B. A khaki armband bearing the Royal Crown was to be provided to all who had enlisted or who had been rejected. This was designed to avoid difficulties with the giving of 'white feathers'. The enlistees were assigned to one of 46 age groups consisting of married or unmarried men. They were told that only entire groups would be called for active service, and that single men's groups would be called before married groups. Anyone marrying after the start of the scheme was classified as single. Tom Watts joined up under this scheme.

The survey was a huge undertaking and was carried in November and December 1915 in a remarkably efficient way. It identified nearly 320,000 medically fit single men. However, 38% of single men and 54% of married men publicly refused to enlist. Examples of posters using a range of subtle, and not so subtle, ways of encouraging men to enlist including phrases such as: "Are you to be handed down to posterity as a Rotter and a Coward?"

ARE YOU A MAN
OR
ARE YOU A MOUSE?
Are you a man who will for ever be handed down to posterity as a Gallant Patriot,
OR
Are you to be handed down to posterity as a Rotter and Coward?
If you are a Man,
NOW
is your opportunity of proving it, and ENLIST at once and go to the nearest Recruiting Officer.
REMEMBER
if you can get 15, 30, or 60 of your Comrades to join, you can all ENLIST together, remain, train, and fight together.
THE COUNTIES—CUMBERLAND AND WESTMORLAND—HAVE
ALWAYS
BEEN CELEBRATED FOR THE FINEST MEN, THE GREATEST SPORTSMEN, AND THE BEST SOLDIERS.
NOW IS YOUR OPPORTUNITY OF PROVING IT.
HURRY UP!
Please take my humble Advice before it is too late.
THE COUNTRY HAS NEVER BEEN IN GREATER PERIL.
LONSDALE,
Lowther Castle.

WOMEN OF BRITAIN
SAY–
"GO!"

COME ON BOYS!
J. S. Watkins.
GIVE US A HAND!

WHO'S ABSENT?
Is it You?

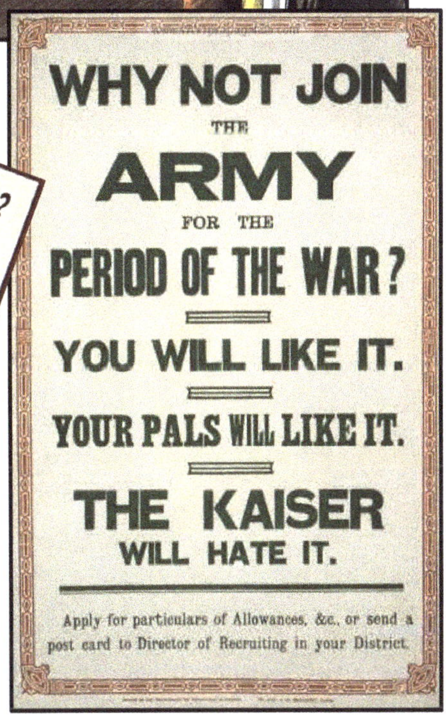
WHY NOT JOIN
THE
ARMY
FOR THE
PERIOD OF THE WAR?
YOU WILL LIKE IT.
YOUR PALS WILL LIKE IT.
THE KAISER
WILL HATE IT.
Apply for particulars of Allowances, &c., or send a post card to Director of Recruiting in your District.

Other methods were used to 'encourage' recruitment. In August 1914, at the beginning of the war, Admiral Fitzgerald founded the Order of the White Feather with the support of the prominent author, Mrs Humphry Ward. This organisation aimed to shame men into enlisting in the British army by women presenting them with a white feather if they were not wearing a uniform. The campaign had mixed success and it was not popular with serving soldiers who might receive a white feather when home on leave from the Front and dressed in their 'civvies' (civilian clothes). Possibly the most inappropriate use of a white feather was the one presented to Seaman George Samson when he was in civilian clothes on his way to a public reception in his honour. Samson had served in the Gallipoli Campaign and had been awarded the Victoria Cross for gallantry.

The Military Service Act 1916

The Government was severely disappointed at the results of the Derby Scheme which did not meet the manpower needs of the Army following the substantial losses on the Western Front. The resulting manpower needed for the army would never be met using the volunteer Derby scheme.

The Government therefore responded by introducing the Military Service Act on 27 January 1916. All voluntary enlistment was stopped. All British males were now deemed to have enlisted on 2 March 1916 – that is, they were *conscripted* – if:

- they were aged between 19 and 41
- they resided in Great Britain excluding Ireland
- they were unmarried or a widower on 2 November 1915.

This act was extended to married men, and the lower conscription age dropped to 18, on 25th May 1916. The introduction of conscription made it very much more difficult for a recruit to falsify his age and name.

A system of appeals tribunals was established, to hear cases of men who believed they were disqualified on the grounds of ill-health, occupation or conscientious objection. Some trades were deemed to be vital to the war economy at home: these were specified as 'starred occupations'.

From September 1916, men who were called up were first assigned to a unit of the Training Reserve. It had been found that the traditional regimental training process was not keeping pace with the flood of men coming through. Therefore the Training Reserve was established to address this issue.

A further extension of the Military Service Act on 10th April 1918 increased the maximum age of recruitment to 50. In addition it allowed soldiers aged 18 years and 6 months to be sent overseas as long as they had had six months training. This decision was triggered by a serious political crisis about the shortage of manpower in France. The shortage was cited as a key reason for the defeat of the Fifth Army in March 1918 during the German Spring offensive.

Formal conscription ceased on 11th November 1918. Any conscripts, who had not already been discharged, were finally released from service on 31st March 1920.

THE SINKING OF THE ARAGON

The RMS Aragon was originally a passenger liner built in Belfast by Harland and Wolff, and was launched on 23rd February 1905 by the Countess Fitzwilliam. For the first few years the ship was operated by the Royal Mail Steam Packet Company as their first 'A-liner, working regular routes between Southampton and South American ports.

After the turn of the century, there had been a serious arms race between Great Britain and Germany, particularly centred on naval power. About three years before the start of WW1, British Intelligence became aware that the German Empire was secretly arming some of its passenger liners. In response, towards the end of 1912 the Admiralty decided also to arm some British passenger liners, starting with RMS Aragon. In April 1913 Aragon left Southampton as Britain's first Defensively Armed Merchant Ship (DAMS), carrying two 4.7-inch naval guns on her stern. She was followed by other 'A class' ships including the Amazon and Alcantara.

HMT Aragon in dock

In the early weeks of the War the Aragon was requisitioned by the Royal Navy and became the RMT Aragon. Its primary role was that of a troopship, and it saw significant service in the Gallipoli campaign both in the initial landings and in the subsequent withdrawal.

In late 1917, the Aragon was assigned to carry reinforcements to the Middle East to support the campaign in Mesopotamia. The troops travelled overland to Southern France to board the ship in Marseilles. Having been two weeks at anchor in December 1917, the Aragon departed Marseille for Egypt via Malta, with another transport ship, the Nile. They were accompanied by an escort group of destroyers. Aragon was carrying some 2500 bags of Christmas mail, 160 Nursing VADs (Voluntary Aid Detachment), 150 military officers, 2200 troops, plus ship's officers and crew.

The Voluntary Aid Detachment was a very successful example of the volunteering spirit of WW1. Over the course of the war, there were over 90,000 women volunteers who worked at home and abroad. They provided vital aid to naval and military forces, caring for sick and wounded sailors and soldiers. Many had specialist training and the VADs, as they became known, served in many of the theatres of war as illustrated by one of their recruitment posters.

Accommodation on board the Aragon was strictly allocated by rank. Non-Commissioned Officers and other ranks were assigned below decks and the upper decks were reserved for the officers and VAD Nurses. The convoy experienced no difficulties on the way to Malta and arrived safely just in time for Christmas. The ship anchored at Windy Bay, where the two transports stayed for four or five days, held up by gale force winds. While there, they celebrated Christmas, and according to one VAD who wrote to her mother, 'Those aboard Aragon had a "top hole" time.'

The Aragon and Nile left Malta with a new escort, HMS Attack and also two Japanese destroyers. According to reports the trip was uneventful and, approaching Alexandria, in northern Egypt, the convoy split with the Nile proceeding to Port Said with the two Japanese destroyers and the Aragon being protected by HMS Attack.

Some accounts report that the Aragon was allowed to enter the Port of Alexandria early on Sunday morning, 30th December 1917, but was ordered back out from the port, either because there was no berth available, or that the harbour was mined. Records vary on this point. Whatever the reason, the Aragon left Alexandria harbour and was stood off at sea, approximately 10 miles from port, when a submarine was sighted which then fired a torpedo. Efforts made to avoid the torpedo were unsuccessful, and the Aragon was hit on the after port side of the ship causing extensive damage to her almost empty aft hold. She immediately began sinking.

HMS Attack and the armed trawler HMT Points Castle came to the rescue. Fortunately there were also other local trawlers in the vicinity. The VADs were ordered into the first lifeboats, albeit under protest, with one VAD being heard to plead "Let us take our chance with the Tommies."

The scene was described in the diary of one of the VADs, Kit Dodsworth, who wrote: 'I was in the social hall talking to Colonel French and Major McLeod when suddenly there was a terrific crash and a lot of dust and bits of wood were blown up into the air over the aft well-deck....The Fall In sounded, we put on our lifebelts and went to our places. There was no panic, although we could feel the ship begin to list a bit. Major McLeod...ragged us like anything as we got into the boat and went down leaving the men all there on deck. They stood there at attention and actually saluted us.'

Attack now drew close alongside Aragon to take survivors aboard as quickly as possible by setting up lines cast between the two ships. The troop ship sank rapidly by the stern making transfer increasingly difficult. A newspaper later reported that the waiting soldiers waiting on deck to be rescued started singing. One said "I have heard the chorus 'Keep the Home Fires Burning' on many occasions but I don't think that I have ever heard it given with so much power".

Only 15 minutes after being struck by the torpedo, the Aragon finally started going down, and the front of the ship came right up out of the water making it impossible to launch any life rafts. Her Master, Captain Bateman, gave the order from the bridge "Every man for himself and God be with you". Those remaining aboard rushed to get over her side. Men poured down the side straight into the sea. Kit Dodsworth described the scene in her diary as a 'swarm of khaki all down the side'. She feared they would not all get off before the ship went down altogether and felt that her friends were drowning before her very eyes.

Illustrated London News 23rd February 1918 with the caption:
The Aragon heeling over before the final plunge: A rescuing destroyer alongside: Soldiers on a life raft from the ship

Most of the VAD nurses transferred to nearby trawlers, from where they watched the tragic scene unfold. Some were transferred to the escort ship HMS Attack. One of these was observed by Driver Bevan who later wrote to his friends in Pontypool saying, "We ought to be proud of our women! I did not see one girl give way. One nurse dived overboard from the Attack exclaiming "I must help the Tommies" She swam about until she had rescued about a dozen men." He added "There is only one country that breeds such women." Although reported in the Illustrated London News, Saturday 23rd February 1918 this was one of many heroic acts that passed without official recognition. In contrast, one soldier, Sergeant Harold Riddlesworth of the Cheshire Regiment, also dived from the same destroyer into the sea to rescue more of the survivors. He survived and was decorated with the Meritorious Service Medal.

Many men probably owed their lives to the new lifejackets that were in use on the Aragon. The Boddy lifejacket was originally invented by George Mallory Boddy in 1914. It was designed to keep the wearer afloat and face upwards. One of the sailors, E G Ware, a Southampton man, described his experiences in the Hampshire Independent on 23rd February 1918:

> 'I cannot swim and without a doubt I owe my life to the Boddy life-saving jacket I was wearing. My station was on the bridge with the skipper, and he sent me down to the engine room to see how things were, the telephone having broken down. When I got back the ship was sinking rapidly. I had on my jacket, and I jumped into the water from a height of thirty or forty feet. At first I felt dazed, but finding the jacket so well supported me, I soon recovered confidence and was able to swim about and escape danger of wreckage which many times threatened. I observed many injured soldiers floating about, quite helpless, wearing their Boddy jackets and their heads well out of the water.....The Boddy jackets had been served in place of the old cork jackets at the beginning of the trip. (Many) were picked up by the destroyer which came to the rescue. Safe on deck, many of them threw their jackets to other men in the water not similarly provided. Then the destroyer was torpedoed in turn and that is where so many lives were lost. I suppose I was in the water for about half-an-hour before I was picked up and, as far as circumstances would admit, quite comfortable. There is no question about it, those jackets saved scores of lives.'

VAD Kit Dodsworth continued her own account and described her time in the lifeboat. 'We landed in the water with a tremendous bump and a huge splash. The crew got hold of the oars and called for someone to take the tiller. I grabbed hold of it but I had no idea of where to steer for. The destroyer was standing by but I noticed that by then some trawlers were coming up and one was as near to us as the destroyer, so I decided to go for that, for the simple reason that it looked as if it would be much easier to get on board. When we got there, the sailors hauled us on board, and the boat went straight back to the ship to pick up some more.'

Just a few minutes later there was a second explosion. It is not clear from the accounts whether this was a second torpedo from the submarine, or the ship's boilers exploding when the cold seawater reached them. Either way the Aragon sank rapidly. About 300-400 men made it onto the Attack.

Only a few moments later tragedy struck again. The Attack itself was then struck by a torpedo in the oil bunkers, which split the ship in two and both sections sank within five to seven minutes. The oil bunkers were ruptured and spilt hundreds of tons of thick bunker fuel oil onto the sea surface. There were hundreds of men in the water, those who had leapt there from the Aragon, and those from the Attack itself, many of whom had the terrifying misfortune of being sunk twice in the space of an hour. Men were coated in the thick black oil or were overcome by the fumes. Many had got wet when the Aragon had sunk and had removed their sodden clothing only to be plunged naked into the oily sea when the Attack sank. Kit Dodsworth recorded that it had been terrible to see what happened to the two mighty ships, which became nothing more than floating wreckage amidst hundreds of swimming soldiers and sailors.

Aragon's surviving lifeboats ferried hundreds of survivors to the trawlers, where the VADs worked tirelessly to tend the many wounded. Other trawlers came out to assist and worked ceaselessly to pick up all the remaining survivors and transfer them to dry land.

The trawler that Kit Dodsworth reached was soon full of rescued troops. She wrote: 'Our own boat was full of men who had been picked up out of the water. Most of them were wet and everything they had on them was wet too. They were pulling little sopping packets of cigarettes out of their pockets. Fortunately, before I had left my cabin I had slipped a full box of a hundred Royal Beauty cigarettes into my pocket, so I handed them round and a sailor followed me with matches'.

‘One poor Jock had had to take off his kilt while he was in the water, because he couldn’t swim with the heavy weight of the material about him. He was sitting shivering in just his wet shirt, looking somewhat ill-at-ease and one of the other VADs noticed his plight. I saw her disappear behind the back of one of the Nurse Sisters and then pop out and hand something to the Jock. When we eventually reached the harbour at Alexandria he went ashore more-or-less decently clad in a pair of ladies silk stockinette knickers.’

Over the hours to come many more rescue trips were made by the trawlers despite the ongoing threat of the submarine. Over two thousand men and women were rescued from the two ships but the death toll was great. The losses on the Aragon were communicated to the House of Commons on 23rd January and confirmed in a statement from the Admiralty on 30th January. The fatalities were: Officers 4 (including the Captain), crew 15, military officers 10, and men 581. Total fatalities: 610. Most of the bodies recovered from the sea were buried in the Alexandria War Memorial Cemetery and their names are recorded on the Chatby War Memorial.

Aragon's second officer was among the survivors. Sometime later he told the master of an Australian troopship, HMAT Indarra, that, before the Aragon went down, Captain Bateman shouted from the bridge to Attack's commander that he would demand an enquiry to explain why his ship had been ordered out of port. Bateman then jumped overboard and was not seen again.

The sinking of the troopship HMT Aragon and its escort destroyer HMS Attack was a serious incident in the history of the U-boat campaign in WW1. Together with the loss of the supply ship HMS Osmanieh, the 48 hours of 30/31st December 1917 were dark times for the British Army and Navy. The ships had been sunk by U-boat UC34 commanded by Horst Obermüller. This U-boat was also responsible for the placing of a mine which HMS Osmanieh struck in the entrance to Alexandria only the day after the Aragon and Attack were sunk. In total, under the command of Horst Obermuller, UC34 sank 7 British ships and damaged one more in the period September 1917 to April 1918.

Horst Obermuller, U Boat Commander and his submarine UC34

The VADs were taken to the Khedivial Hotel which was serving as a billet for nursing staff. Most had lost everything in the sinking and only had the clothes they stood up in. On New Year's Eve they were given an allowance to shop for necessities and then reported for duty the following day, New Year's Day 1918, barely 48 hours after being torpedoed and rescued at sea. Troops were taken to holding camps before re-deployment. Many of the survivors from Aragon's crew were repatriated to England, reaching Southampton on 10th February 1918.

News of the tragedy only became public over time. As stated in the Army and Navy Gazette of 9th Saturday February 1918, Dr. Macnamara, MP for Camberwell North, confirmed that 'The public notification of the losses of these vessels was being delayed until all the relatives had been notified. This course had been adopted because it was found that immediate notification in the Press immediately about incidents and losses gave rise to the greatest anxiety amongst families and communities. Relatives could be left in doubt as to whether members of their family circle serving on those vessels might be amongst those lost.'

The Admiralty on Jan. 30 issued the following:—

The transport *Aragon* (Captain Francis Bateman in command) was torpedoed and sunk in the Eastern Mediterranean on Dec. 30. One of his Majesty's destroyers, whilst picking up the survivors from the *Aragon*, was herself torpedoed and sunk, as reported in the *communiqué* of Jan. 7. The Mercantile Fleet Auxiliary *Osmanieh* (Lieut.-Commander D. R. Mason, R.N.R., in command) struck a mine and sank in approximately the same locality on Dec. 31. The casualties were as follows:—*Aragon*: Officers, 4 (including the Captain); crew, 15; military officers, 10; men, 581. *Osmanieh*: Officers, 3 (including the Captain); crew, 21; military officer, 1; men, 166; female nurses, 8.

The foregoing information was communicated to the House of Commons on Jan. 23, in reply to a question from Mr. Houston, by Dr. Macnamara, who added: The public notification of the losses of these vessels was being delayed until all the relatives had been notified. This course had been adopted because they found that notification in the Press immediately upon the loss gave rise to the greatest anxiety amongst members of the community who, from the area in which their relatives were serving, were left in doubt as to whether members of their family circle might not be amongst those lost.

The Army and Navy Gazette
9th February 1918

This explains why Lizzie personally heard that Fred was safe before the sinking was widely known, and the Surrey Herald was then able to report on his safety (18th January) before the national newspapers, which mainly covered the story in the period from 30th/31st January onwards when the news was generally released.

THE PEOPLE, SUNDAY, FEBRUARY 3, 1918. 7

LONDON: STORIES OF SUNK TRANSPORTS.

SEVEN FIREMEN KILLED.

COLLAPSE OF FOUR WALLS.

JUDGE'S DESPAIR.

STATE OFFICIAL WHO GOT A BETTER JOB.

BOMBS ON PARIS.

YOUNG HUN BARONS.

GERMAN "REPRISAL."

COMMONS v. PEERS.

"P.R." Proposal Deleted From Franchise Bill.

BRITISH TROOPSHIP TORPEDOED.

HOW THE ARAGON, WITH 2,500 ON BOARD, WENT TO HER DOOM.

Details are now available of the loss of the troopship Aragon, which was torpedoed in the Eastern Mediterranean on Dec. 30. She had about [illegible] troops on board, and the death roll was 610. One of H.M. destroyers, while picking up survivors, was herself torpedoed and sunk.

A day later the mercantile fleet auxiliary Osmanieh struck a mine in the same locality and sank. In this case the losses were 196, including eight female nurses.

The Cunard liner Andania has been torpedoed and sunk off the Ulster coast. All on board, save two, were saved.

Once again the return of merchant shipping losses from mines and U-boats is satisfactory, only nine big and six small vessels being sunk. It is now generally conceded that many U-boats have been temporarily withdrawn to their bases for refitting preparatory to embarking on a far-reaching campaign of destruction.

THE LOST TRANSPORTS.

Doomed Soldiers Go Down Singing.

A Nurse's Narrative.

CUNARDER SUNK.

Andania Hit Amidships: Only Two Missing.

U-BOAT TOLL.

The sinking of the Aragon makes the national press

The People Sunday 3rd February 1918

An artist's impression of the Sinking of the Aragon. by the well-known maritime artist Charles Dixon (1872-1934)
Published in The Graphic Saturday 9th February 1918

LIZZIE - THE FIRE

"It was the most dreadful night of my life. I don't know how I got through it and all the aftermath. I never knew you could hurt so much without dying. But I'm getting ahead of myself. There are things to say before the events of that night. I have just the one photograph of Syd from around this time and I do treasure it as a lasting momento. He was always such a handsome man to me.

Syd Watts

Syd had worked at Madeley's the grocers for around 35 years, ever since he were a lad. That's how we met as I told you earlier. He started as a porter's assistant and gradually worked his way up until he was what they called a grocer's traveller. This meant he went round the big houses outside the town checking and talking through the weekly, and often twice weekly, grocery orders with the domestic staff, taking their requirements back to the store, supervising the making up of the order ready for delivering them. He was happy in his work and it was stable and secure work which was such a blessing as we had so many children to feed.

Of course, the war started to change all this. Food shortages were common and unpredictable. We managed quite well as Syd had dug up the whole of the back garden and turned it into our own allotment growing a lot of vegetables that we needed. I'd cultivated the front garden just like other wives in the road. By the start of 1918, rationing and ration books had been introduced. Then the Food Committee banned the delivery of all meats and made everyone go in person to collect their rations from the shop where they were registered. So Syd's job at Madeleys all but disappeared almost overnight. We knew things were tight at the stores because there weren't the same range of food and groceries for them to sell so turnover was down. Mr Madeley moved Syd to working at the warehouse. At least he kept a job. But it was much harder work, lifting and lugging sacks all day. His health wasn't what it was, and his heart was getting weaker and sometimes he fought for breath although he were only in his middle fifties.

He quickly but reluctantly decided he needed a different job and wanted something that would help the war effort. Just by coincidence a job came up at Watneys in Weybridge, the munitions and aeronautical engineers. It was Major Watney who raised the ASC division that our Sydie had joined in 1915. Anyway Syd applied and got the job with the help of very good references from Mr Madeley. He started early in March but the overnight hours were long. He started at 6.30 in the evening and clocked off 12 hours later, getting home just in time for breakfast. It was such a change for our daily routine so the children had to keep quiet when Syd was sleeping in the day.

It had been a difficult start to the Spring that year. Syd lost both his Mother and his eldest brother within two weeks of each other. Syd's mother, Eliza, was still living in Chertsey when she passed away in early March. We'd barely been to the funeral and buried her when we heard that Syd's brother Henry had taken a turn for the worse and died in Southwark. Henry hadn't been well enough to come to his mother's funeral in Chertsey so perhaps it wasn't unexpected. These deaths hit my Syd hard cos he'd always been so close to his mother and looked up to Henry who was the eldest in the family. Syd had done so much to care for his mother and see she was alright after his father died way back in 1899. He seemed so very sad and it was hard to raise his spirits, because like me, he was also so worried about the lads serving in the Army. It really all seemed to get on top of him which was really unusual as he had been such a bold outgoing man all his life.

At first all was well with the new job. Syd did get really excited when King George V and Queen Mary visited Watneys at the end of April to open the new Canteen Theatre. It really buoyed his spirits after the family deaths. The theatre was quite the talking point with the families of the women who worked there. There was even, what they called, an artist in residence who sketched and painted scenes from the daily life at the factory.

Visit of King George V and Queen Mary to Watney's Factory
April 1918

And then, only a couple of weeks later, came that night, that dreadful fateful night, the 9th May. And all only a fortnight since we'd heard that Sydie was safe in Malta after the Cameronia was sunk. A Thursday it was. It had just been a lovely warm sunny day without a hint of the darkness that was to descend on us all. I'd been working at the Surrey Herald Office until the middle of the afternoon and then home for the usual chores.

It was just before midnight, when we were all abed and sound asleep, and suddenly there was the most almighty continuing banging on the front door. It just carried on and on and we all heard a man shouting "Wake up Mrs Watts. Wake up! It's an emergency. Come and open the door!" I stuck my head out of the front bedroom window and called "Who's there? What on earth's the matter?"

"It's George, George Baker. I work with Syd at Watneys. Come down and open the door, quick! Please!" I was really alarmed by this and threw on my dressing gown and dashed down the stairs. By this time all the rest of the house were awake and coming down behind me. I threw open the door and George nearly fell so eager was he to get in.

"It's Syd," he gasped. There's been a fire and he's hurt. He's alive but he's injured. They've taken him to Weybridge Cottage Hospital. Major Watney has sent a motorcar for you, to take you to the hospital but be quick please," I could see the tears in his eyes and this made me so scared. "What's happened? Is he alright?"

"No time for that now. Get some clothes on and I'll tell you on the way" I rushed upstairs and dressed calling instructions to Ruth to look after Alice and Lawrence, telling her I'd be back as soon as possible. "Anything happens, go to the Smiths next door" I thought they'd all be awake anyway with all the noise George had made.

I'd never been in a proper motorcar before; just wishing it wasn't in these circumstances. George said it was one of Major Watney's Mercedes that he used to sell before the war. Thinking back now, I guess there wasn't too much call for German cars after 1914. I do remember it was noisy and bumpy but much quicker than anything else for getting to the hospital. On the way George told me what he knew had happened. Apparently Syd had gone to do his evening rounds again about 10.30 then, just moments later, there was a huge explosion and the petrol store was on fire along with other buildings. "We tried to contain the fire but it was so hot. We dragged Syd clear away from the flames but he's been burnt. I don't know how badly but the ambulance came quite quick and took him to Weybridge. Fire engines have been there from Addlestone, Weybridge and Chertsey. Fire's under control now."

I just couldn't reply. My head was racing with alarm and fear and all manner of thoughts. I just sat there, feeling so alone. We got to the Cottage Hospital not long after 12.30, according to the clock in thc hospital hall.

"Mrs Watts?" the nurse said. I nodded. "Come with me. I'll take you to him. Doctor has said you were to see him straight away." I noticed Syd was in a separate room, not on a ward. There were two nurses at his bedside but nothing could have prepared me for what I saw – he was bandaged round his head and you could see where he had been bleeding. He was so blackened by the smoke but there were clean areas where the nurses had been working on his burns. Oh what a terrible sight. He was unconscious and looked barely alive. "How is he?" I managed to blurt out. "Will he live?"

I felt a hand softly on my shoulder and turned to see a Doctor in a white coat. "I'm Dr Wilson and I treated your husband when he was admitted. Just come with me and we can talk and I'll try to answer your questions." Oh, I remember he was a lovely man with such gentle eyes.

We went into the corridor and sat down on two chairs. "It's not good I'm afraid. He has a bad injury to his head and some very nasty burns all down his left side. He hasn't regained consciousness since the explosion. We've stopped the bleeding and made him as comfortable as we can. We have to let nature take its course and pray. But you should prepare yourself for the worst. I'm so sorry." I didn't know what to say, what to feel or how to react. There were no words. Eventually, I think I said something like "Thank you Doctor. Can I go and sit by him"

"Yes, I think you should. It would be good if you talk to him"

I sat by his bed for I don't know how long, holding his right hand which hadn't been burnt. The nurses came and went. Some others from Watneys came and asked about Syd and then went and waited in the corridor.

My poor darling Syd never stirred. His eyelids were still and the room was silent. I don't know if he ever heard the things I said to him but I prayed he did. All the things I wish I'd said to him but never did – so I tried to say them then.

And then it happened, around 3.30 in the morning according to the nurse. He quietly slipped away; he didn't seem to be in pain. He just stopped breathing and passed over. I felt his hand go limp and then my tears really came. I thought they'd never stop. By this time others of the family had arrived.

The rest is just a blur. I can't remember it clearly even after all these years. I suppose we got home and then got caught up in telling the family, and then making arrangements for the funeral. But before the funeral, first came the inquest on the Monday. This was just a blur again for me. I do remember that it rained all day – a dismal, dreary day for a dreadful event. I kept the newspaper report and it's best if you just read that. I couldn't remember all the details. Though what I do remember was the great kindness that the members of the jury showed me. They all chose to donate their fees and gave them to me and the family. It was unasked but it was so very touching.

We buried Syd at Chertsey Cemetery. There was a huge turnout. It had drizzled in the morning but the weather broke for the burial and we laid Syd to rest under sunny skies. All the Watts's were there and so many other people from the town and beyond. The tragedy had been quite the talk of the town and had been in all the newspapers. There was so much love and respect for Syd that it strangely made the funeral and burial a little easier to live through.

THE FUNERAL

The funeral took place at Chertsey Cemetery on Thursday afternoon, and was attended by members of the Order of Foresters, munition girls, and some of the night staff at Mssrs. Gordon Watney and Co.'s works. Mr. R. W. Eglan represented the firm. Mr. H. J. Madeley, by whom the deceased was employed for 37 years, was also present. Among those sending wreaths were Major Gordon Watney, the watchmen at the South Lodge Works, the staff at Madeley's, fellow workers at Watney's etc. There was a service at St. Peter's Church, conducted by the Rev. H. Heath who also officiated at the cemetery.

Copy of Funeral Report of Death of Sydney Watts (Senior)
Died 10th May 1918 - Buried 14th May 1918

ADDLESTONE
ALARMING FIRE AT MUNITION WORKS
NIGHT WATCHMAN'S DEATH

On Thursday night, between 10 and 11 o'clock, residents of Weybridge, Addlestone and Chertsey heard a terrific explosion, which, it was afterwards ascertained, came from the cleaning shed at the works of Mssrs. Gordon Watney and Co., Addlestone. The night watchman, Sidney Watts, of Grove Road, Chertsey, had apparently entered the shed shortly before the explosion. Many of the men on night shift rushed towards the building, and some of them pluckily managed to bring Watts out in a dying condition, being themselves burnt whilst doing so. The shed is fortunately practically isolated, with brick wall on one side of it.

Telephone messages were at once sent for neighbouring fire brigades, and Weybridge, Addlestone and Chertsey firemen, with their engines, were soon at the works, and promptly played on the building, from which volumes of flames were issuing. Chertsey received the call at about ten minutes to 11, and with their motor engine, under Captain Perrow, made a record journey, although on arrival they found the other two brigades already at work under their respective captains.

The Chertsey men ran a hose for some hundreds of yards from the adjacent canal, and plenty of water was available. Working methodically and with much coolness the firemen prevented the flames extending, and after some hours all further danger was over.

The cleaning shed contained much petrol and the explosion was one of great violence, but no explanation can be given of the cause. The damage is considerable.

Watts, the watchman, was for 33 years employed as Mssrs. Madeley's grocery establishment, Chertsey, and only recently resigned there to go the munitions works.

Copy of Report of Munitions Fire at Watney & Co.
Surrey Advertiser, Monday 13th `May 1918

Fortunately Tom and Albert came home on leave not long after the funeral. The first time I'd seen them in nearly twenty months. It was some comfort to have them back and giving me their support and at times a much needed shoulder to cry on. I tried not to cry as 'Life had to go on somehow'. Well it had to with the younger children still at home who needed me to provide for them and to bring them up having so suddenly lost their Father.

After the tragedy folk in the neighbourhood and in the town were very kind and very thoughtful. People called in to see how I was and to just have a chat. It all helped to fill my days in between caring for the children who were still at home and as well as carrying on with my job. It was in the quiet times or when I was talking with family that the questions came. 'Why did he have to change his job? Why didn't he just stay on at Madeley's? Why didn't I stop him moving? Could we have found another way of coping?'

Then I'd think about the fire and yet more questions would come. 'He was always so careful, how could it have happened? Why did he have a lantern when there was petrol in the sheds? Shouldn't they have thought of that? Why did he check that shed?' But I did know the answer to that last one. Syd was always so conscientious and I knew he wouldn't have skipped anything that was his responsibility to do.

Then my mind would get round to thinking about all the things I might have said to him but didn't and regret for the few cross words we ever had. But then I'd right myself and think instead of all the good times we'd had. Remembering when we were courting and when we got married; our wonderful children and how they had grown up as young men and women to be proud of especially our four sons away fighting for their King and Country.

What I did know was that life must go on. Not as I had imagined it would be, growing old together and watching our grandchildren play and grow up. I knew it had to be a different future, on my own but with my family; choosing and making my own path forward. Doing what my mother had drummed into me, 'Women have to be strong. You find your own way in life. If you get knocked down, you pick yourself up and you carry on.'

So with these words ringing in my head, I tried to face forwards, looking forward to the end of the war which surely couldn't be long now, especially now that the Americans had joined in. And of course looking forward to peace when life could get back to something that we remembered and treasured. I can't say it was easy. I did so miss my Syd but there was no other way but forward, you can't just live in the past. I could see the dangers of that with so many mothers and wives in the town who had lost their husbands and sons in the war. I decided to concentrate on what my family would all be doing after the war was over, their new jobs, marriages for the younger ones, grandchildren to come – a new generation to take us all forward.

Soon all my four brave lads were home. Demobbed, having done their duty and able to hold their heads high. They'd been sent to countries none of them would have imagined visiting, been wounded, sunk at sea, had terrible diseases, had medals for bravery, seen things no man should ever have to see and of course experienced things they would probably never talk about. But they were all back and all safe. Their faces were more lined and careworn but their smiles were the same. Their sense of humour, especially Albert and Fred, was even sharper than before and they had some wonderfully funny and occasionally tragic tales to tell. Sunday tea was never quite the same again. I guess the humour and the jokes were their way of coping and making sense of the horrors they'd lived through. And, I can confidently say, the laughing helped me too. It's very hard to feel down when your sides are aching from one of Albert's tales.

So, with my family around me, I did my best to look to the future and just got on with it. It wasn't the future I'd dreamed off all through the war but that's just how it was. There were changes of course and I planted flowers in the front garden wanting to mark the end of the war and the arrival of the peace that we'd all craved. I'd take some of the flowers with me when I visited Syd and had my little chats with him by his graveside. I felt I wanted to keep him in touch with the family and let him know what was going on. I kept the back garden for growing my own vegetables as I needed this to supplement my money as much as a memorial for Syd who had devoted so many hours to it. Edith and Reg lived with me so we managed a household budget and got by. I'll tell you about all the others next."

Report of the Inquest Proceedings

Transcript of leading article in Surrey Herald. 17th May 1918

FATAL FIRE AT MUNITION WORKS

Inquest on Chertsey Man Killed at Gordon Watney's.

The sequel to the unfortunate fire at Messrs.Gordon Watney and Co's aeronautical engineering works was held at the Board Room, Weybridge Cemetery, on Monday afternoon, when Mr. Gilbert White conducted the inquest on the body of the victim - Mr. Sydney Watts, a night watchman living at Grove Road, Chertsey, and 55 years of age.

About 10.45 p.m. on Thursday last a loud explosion had startled the neighbourhood. It was the explosion of the petrol stores, and Mr Watts, who had just closed the doorway of the building, was hurled to the ground and pinned there by a portion of the fallen wall. The alarm was immediately raised, and several employees did their utmost to rescue the unfortunate man and also retard the progress of the flames, which could be seen for miles around.

Obstacles were placed between the raging furnace and the prostrate injured man, but it was some time before he could be extricated, and he succumbed to his burns and injuries at 3.30 in Weybridge hospital. In the meantime the local firemen had been exceptionally busy and a remarkable measure of success attended their efforts. Beyond the petrol stores, the fire was confined to the cleaning-down shed (where engines back from France and other fronts are stripped for repair). These two buildings were devoured by the fire, but all the other huge shops in close proximity remained intact. It was a performance upon which the local brigades deserved every commendation. The Weybridge men, with their motor engine and under C.O. Wood, were first on the scene, and Chertsey, under C.O. Perrow, did so well that they were on the spot before Addlestone, although the latter were considerably nearer.

Mr. Watts had been with the firm only since March, for 35 years prior to which he was with Messrs. E T. and H. J. Madeley, grocers, Chertsey. Several men were burned in attempting his rescue, among them being Mr. Shepherd, a night foreman and one who took part in the Retreat from Mons. A prominent part in his eventual release was taken by Mr. Barnett, of Albert Road, Addlestone.

EVIDENCE AT THE INQUEST (SURREY HERALD REPORT CONTINUED)

M. P. T. Berryman legally represented Messrs. Gordon Watney and Co. at the inquest on Monday, and Mr. W. Rambridge was foreman of the jury. Major Gordon Watney and Mr. H. Beverley (H. M. Inspector of Factories) were also present.

Evidence of identification was given by George Baker, ex-Sergeant in the Surrey Constabulary, living at Guildford Road, Chertsey, and now employed as a night time keeper and watchman by the firm. Witness and deceased went on duty on Thursday evening at 6.30, and remained together until 10.30, when Mr. Watts commenced the first round of clocking - inspecting the various buildings, in which his time was recorded by a system of clocks. He went through the machine shops and the offices upstairs, and after putting on his overcoat at the time office, proceeded to the works on the other side of the yard. That was the last witness saw of him alive. A minute or two after deceased left the time office he (Baker) heard a loud explosion. Running into the yard, he found that the petrol stores were ablaze. Almost immediately he met Mr. Eglon, who summoned the local fire brigades.

Answering the Coroner, witness said that deceased was carrying a lamp which might be described as a policeman's bull's-eye oil lamp.

Mr. W. R. Eglon, secretary of Messrs Gordon Watney and Co said that we was in the house which is on the premises and he heard the explosion. Upon ascertaining the cause he immediately telephoned for the brigades. The petrol stores were completely demolished, as also was one other building, He believed that at the time about 1,000 gallons of petrol were in store; the quantity allowed by the license of the Chertsey Council was 1,500 gallons. Deceased, in the course of his rounds, would have to enter the petrol stores, for the purpose of clocking.

Mr. Eglon produced the clock carried by the deceased in his rounds on the fatal evening showing by the chart that the petrol store had been clocked. The leather case of the clock had been burned - Mr. Beverley and the Coroner, reading from the regulations attached to the license, said that no artificial fire or light was permitted "to be carried into or near the store at any time." The foreman of the jury thought that the standard for the clock might preferably have been placed outside the building, and so avoided the necessity of his entrance.

Mr. Baker, recalled, said the lamp was not carried into the petrol stores. The deceased usually placed it on the ground outside when he entered. The door of the petrol store opened inwards. They would not carry a lamp inside. There was an electric light switch within the stores. Richard Barnett, of 25, Albert Road, Addlestone, said he hurried to the works hearing the explosion. Close by the where the door of the petrol stores had been Mr. Watts was lying on the ground, face upwards with the lower portion of his body covered by the debris, including the door of the wrecked building. Several unsuccessful attempts were made before he was pulled out by means of a rope.

Sgt. Daws, Addlestone, spoke to being close to the works at the time of the explosion. The petrol spread to the breaking-up shed which also became involved. Several attempts were made before deceased was got away with the aid of a scaffold cord.

The lamp carried by the deceased was in a damaged condition lying to his left, and quite close to where the door had stood. Later the lock of the door was found, with the key fixed in it. Locked- showing that the explosion occurred after the door was closed and the key turned, but before the key was extracted.

Dr H. S. Wilson, Weybridge, said he saw the deceased at the Weybridge Cottage Hospital about 11.30, when he was very seriously injured and obviously dying. The whole of the left side of the body was badly burned, and there were all the symptoms of a compound fracture of the base of the skull. Deceased passed away at 3.30 a.m., the cause of death being shock following extensive injuries to the skull and body. In all probability the fracture to the skull was sustained quite early, so that he would be rendered unconscious and helpless, and not feel much of the burning which followed.

Major Gordon Watney offered to give evidence or answer any inquiries, but the Coroner and jury did not deem this to be necessary. Major Watney thereupon mentioned that the clocking arrangements had to be placed well within the buildings, in order that proper inspection could be made. Every care was taken that the watchmen were informed of the danger attached to some buildings such as the petrol stores. If the stores were overloaded with fumes it would be the watchman's duty to leave the door open for 10 minutes or so, and so permit their escape.

The Coroner, in his brief summing up, said the evidence pointed to the fact that the lamp had not been carried inside the building, it was possible that the lamp was placed too near the building, and that the fumes on being fanned outwards to the lamp caused the explosion,

The jury returned a verdict of " Accidental Death," and handed their fees to the fund being raised for the widow.

THE FUNERAL (SURREY HERALD REPORT CONTINUED)

The remains of the deceased were interred in the Chertsey cemetery on Friday afternoon, following a service at St. Peter's Church. The officiating clergyman was the Rev. Huntley Heath, curate-in-charge. Representatives of the Ancient Order of Foresters walked in front of the hearse, and at the rear was a party of male and female munition workers from the night staff of Messrs. Gordon Watney and Co. The firm was represented by Mr. R. W. Eglon (secretary), and among the employees present was Mrs. Pearce (night matron). Mr. H. J. Madeley was also present.

The coffin bore the following inscription: --

Sydney Watts, died May 10th, 1918. Aged 55 years." Wreaths and flowers, in addition to those from the family, were sent by: Major Gordon Watney, the watchmen at South Lodge works, neighbours and friends in Grove Road, staff at Madeley's, fellow-workers at Gordon Watney's, a few friends, in kind and grateful memory of 35 years' faithful service from Mrs. Madeley, senr., and Mr. and Mrs. Harry Madeley.

Mr. P. Percey, of Chertsey, was the undertaker.

Mrs. Watts and family desire to express their gratitude to the large number of persons who expressed sympathy, or forwarded floral tributes, on the occasion of their great bereavement.

A lengthy poem was published in the Surrey Herald about the tragedy.

Reprinted from The Surrey Herald, May 17th.

GORDON WATNEY and CO., LTD.

9th MAY, 1918.

The hour, it was close on mid-night,
The work was going ahead,
When hark! A terrific explosion,
My God! Can it be a raid?

But suddenly through the fanlight,
We could see a flame of gold,
A lurid red in the darkness
We did not need to be told.

Out to the yard we rushed,
And the sight which met us there,
Fascinated and held us
We could only stand and stare.

"The petrol shed's on fire boys,"
Was the cry which rent the air,
"Has anyone seen the watchman?
Why the dickens is he not here?"

Someone rushed to the telephone
Others to quell the flames.
"Every man is needed,
Quick, boys, before it gains!"

Two men came running forward
They call for stretcher and rope,
To save the brave night-watchman,
There is yet a gleam of hope.

After many attempts they rescued
The man from his cruel fate,
To the hospital near they bore him,
But alas! It was all too late.

He died a few hours later,
A hero's unselfish death,
Leaving behind him this memory,
Obedience to duty - and faith.

Meanwhile the men were busy
Clearing engines and petrol away,
Saving as much as possible
Of explosives which round them lay.

Brave lads, they thought not of danger,
Some had seen worse sights before
On the battle fields of Flanders,
In the early days of war.

With the Major at their head,
And the foreman - a Mon's hero,
The work they did was splendid,
And for all the others - Cheero!

The fire brigades from Chertsey,
Weybridge and Addlestone too,
Deserve the highest praise
For the dangers they went through.

We thank Mrs. Pearce, our Matron,
For the work she did that night,
When the girls were fainting round her,
Suffering from shock and fright.

We must not forget the Major,
Before we end this tale,
He showed true British spirit,
By carrying on so well.

The flames were subdued by daylight,
Three cheers for Watney's men;
We hope a similar experience,
May never occur again.

Now we're sure you'll excuse the Triplets
If they bore you with these lines,
But we hope you won't ignore the fact,
We've developed poetic minds.

When we're home in Bonnie Scotland,
Apres this fearful guerre,
We'll never forget G.W. and Co.,
When we were working there.

By

THE "TRIPLETS"

Messrs. Gordon Watney and Co's Hostel, Heath Club, Weybridge.

GORDON WATNEY & CO

Before the Great War, Gordon Watney was the owner of South Lodge Works, a motor engine workshop and dealership for Mercedes cars. The factory specialised in importing Mercedes cars/chassis and putting custom made sports bodies on them. These designs attracted a lot of attention and his business was supported by a distinctive advertising campaign. He also raced at Brooklands, Britain's first motor racing circuit which opened in 1907 where it was the world's first purpose-built 'banked' motor racing circuit.

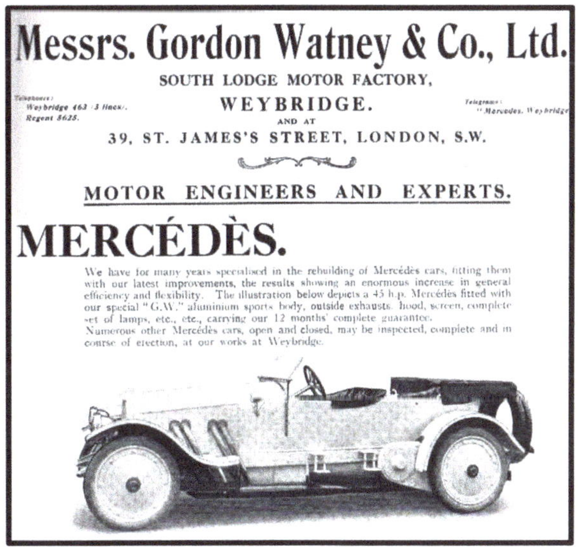

Gordon Watney's advertisements. Above, a more traditional approach and left an example of a more 'flamboyant' approach.

At the start of the war, Gordon Watney refocussed his business into a refurbishment factory for aero engines for the government. In his role as an officer, Major Watney was also commissioned to establish a motor transport company by the War Office. This attracted many local men and became known as the Watney Boys who went onto serve in Mesopotamia and Gallipoli. The refurbishment business proved to be successful and a key support to the growing role of the Royal Flying Corps. On 26th April 1918, this important role of the firm was recognised by King George V and Queen Mary during their visit to the factory.

The factory also became well known being one of the first to have an 'artist in residence'. Nellie Isaac was a painter, illustrator, designer and inventor. Before the war she exhibited at the Royal Academy featuring her watercolours "A Florentine" and "La Blonde". Her work at the factory was initiated by the Imperial War Museum. The Museum was established in 1917, and Agnes Conway – the daughter of the honorary director Sir Martin Conway – was invited to form a Women's Work Sub-Committee, with the aim of capturing and documenting the social change in the lives of women through the war.

Universal conscription had led to women's employment in all kinds of labouring and clerical work previously the domain of men. For example women hauled coal, collected bus fares, mended roads, delivered the post, and also worked on the land and in factories.

Nellie Isaac contacted Sir Martin Conway offering to contribute to the initiative by giving up her art and design business and for two years to work at Gordon Watney's factory. While there she painted a number of works – Scenes from the Canteen Theatre, Sports Day, Receiving News of the Armistice and the Victory celebrations. Interviewed at the time, she said she had wanted "to do something that we felt would be of national importance".

Pictures painted by Nellie Isaac at Gordon Watney's factory
A scene from the theatre established in the factory
On the previous page, women's tug'o'war from the factory sports day

The business suffered a disaster when much of the factory was destroyed in a fire on 9th May 1918 when 107 engines, property of the government, were destroyed. The circumstances of the fire are described in the account of the inquest in the previous section.

The aftermath of the fire became problematic for Watney due to major issues with the insurance claim on the engines and buildings. Apparently he was insured for "fire" but the insurance company claimed that the damage was the result of an "explosion" and declined to pay out. This being despite the evidence provided at the inquest of Sydney Watts, the night-watchman who died as a result of the fire. Additionally, the War department valued the engines at £47,430, but Watney stated that some were not able to be rebuilt and should therefore be valued as scrap, decreasing their value to £31,000. To date no specific records have come to light about how these disputes were resolved.

After the war, Major Watney continued in the motor trade but was apparently not as successful as he had been previously, being recorded as merely an agent of ABC Motors in 1920.

LIZZIE - AFTER THE WAR

"After the Armistice and when all the lads had come home, life slowly began to settle down again. But I still couldn't believe that Syd wasn't there to share the joyous homecoming of all four lads and, of course, Edith's husband Reg, who had also served in France. So many families had lost sons. I was just so thankful for their safe return but it was tinged with sadness every time I thought of my Syd. Oh, if only he hadn't changed jobs. But I know regrets never change anything. My old Mum would have said "Pick yourself up Lizzie and just get on with it"

Even the celebrations for the end of the war and the decorated streets did little to raise my spirits. The town was wonderfully decorated with flags and bunting to acknowledge the end of the fighting. But thinking back, there wasn't quite the same sense of real joy and happiness among the townsfolk that there had been with the old Queen's jubilee. The celebrations were tinged with a sense of utter relief and rescue from the years of worry and fear for all our loved ones. It was almost as though people thought it wouldn't be somehow right to be too happy as there were so many families that had lost husbands, brothers, fathers and sons and for whom the world would never be the same again. You might say it was a polite celebration. That's not to say that weren't those who had a really good time and, of course, the pubs were certainly busy!

Guildford Street after the Armistice 1918

Chertsey Decorated for Victory Celebrations
Bell Corner 1918

My youngest, Fred was the first to come home, though it felt a bit odd as he was the last to join up. That's just the way these things work I suppose. However the others followed very soon after. They all talked about having a future now when they hadn't dared hope for years. They'd all just concentrated on getting through the war. I won't talk about some of the things they said that they'd experienced. Maybe all those things should be quietly laid to rest as the four lads and Reg were all trying to do.

Mind you, it wasn't possible to just put the war from our minds. There were the poor fellows that had been badly wounded, losing an arm or a leg or, maybe worse, I don't know, being disfigured. You saw them about in the town, you felt so sorry for them but they were a permanent reminder – lest we forget.

One of the things I was most proud of came not long after the end of the war. The general election in December 1918 was the first time some women had the vote and I was one of them. I remember standing at the voting booth thinking how proud my Syd would have been. Finally women getting some of the recognition we certainly deserved. Well they couldn't really do otherwise after all we'd done in the war.

We'd been doing men's jobs just as well as them, better some might say. I'd always believed that the time would come when we would be seen as equals. That day was a big step for me and the other women who got the vote. But it wasn't for all women. I qualified because our house was a big enough rateable value or some such unreal measure of a woman's worth. I thought back to the day that there had been a Suffragette meeting in the Town Hall which caused some outcry in the town. Someone managed to get a photograph from the upstairs of Nicholson's the Chemist's and had some postcards printed. It was about the time there was all that trouble about the arson of Sir George White's mansion at Englefield Green. Thinking back, it must have been the year before the War started. Feelings were running very high in the town about the meeting and there was quite a lively crowd outside the Town Hall. I certainly thought it was a good thing that the fight for women's votes had become local.

Crowds outside the Town Hall for the Suffragette Meeting 1913

Anyway, back to the election of 1918, I decided to vote early that day, partly because I couldn't wait to cast my vote after all this time waiting for the right that should have been ours years before. But also because Blanche, next door, was nervous about voting. She only just qualified as being over 30 years of age and was talking to me about it all. So I said, "Let's go early and let's go together. I'm sure we'll figure it out." Well we were early and because it was December, it was still dark but dry. In fact we were the first in line, apart that is from the election officials and one gentleman from the Press who was reporting on the election. Everything went very smoothly with our names being recorded on the registers and being given our ballot paper. I heard afterwards that there was some trouble when a group of women who were registered to vote but had been left off the polling station list – so not everything went well for everybody who were entitled to vote.

LING DISTRICT F. PARISH OF CHERTSEY.
(CHERTSEY WARD).

(1) No.	(2) Names in full. Surname first.	(3) Residence or Property occupied and abode of non-resident occupier.
	GROVE ROAD—*continued.*	
685	Boyd, Margaret Jane	17
686	Gray, Robert Alfred	19
687	Gray, Lottie	19
688	Grinstead, Ann	21
689	Cosson, Jane	22
690	Clark, Horace	23
691	Pain, Henry William	24
692	Pain, Marah	24
693	Smith, Henry	25
694	Smith, Blanche	25
695	Harris, William Samuel	26
696	Harris, Emily Mary	26
697	Watts, Elizabeth	27
698	a Lifford, William	28
699	Lifford, Emma E.	28
700	Tappin, James George	29

Extract from 1919 Electoral Role for Chertsey showing Elizabeth Watts of 27 Grove Road as eligible to vote.

How did I vote? Now I'm not telling you that! It's called a secret ballot for a reason. But I will tell you that I didn't vote for the people who thought they had the right to tell working people what to do and who lived off the backs of others. It was time for a change but it didn't happen then. It was a proud moment stood there with a pencil in my hand but it was sad too. I was doing it on my own, without Syd. I'm a strong woman; always had a mind of my own but he'd been my rock for so many years. It was wonderful to have all the lads home safe but it looked like a long bleak future at that moment without Syd.

Things changed after the War but not back to how it was. It never could. There were too many families still mourning their losses and too many gaps where the menfolk had been. Many of the wartime jobs changed for women as soon as the Act of Parliament made it clear that most women who had been doing the men's jobs had to give them up and hand them back to the returning soldiers and sailors. On the one hand nobody minded that and thought it was only fair given the sacrifice they'd all made. But on the other hand, we women had tasted a different way of life, and we'd been valued for more than just being wives and mothers. It was never going to be the same again. We'd done the jobs that men had done, and done them just as well, and some said better! We were much more confident, more outward going and had greater hopes for our lot in this world.

There were a good number of our lads coming back who found it difficult to get jobs. It was just like the market was flooded all at once. Fate was kind to my lads and they all found work quickly. At least that was one step of getting back to normal.

The unveiling of the War Memorial in Chertsey was a great coming together for the town allowing all of us to celebrate the safe return of our loved ones as well as a chance to mourn the Fallen. It was unveiled at the end of October 1921. The ceremony was attended by Lieutenant Colonel Clare, who lived locally in Chertsey, and also the Bishop of Guildford. I came to see my Syd as one of the Fallen of the Great War, as the dead were commonly called. Most of the family were at the ceremony and Sydle was captured in one of the photographs taken that were then made into postcards.

Ceremony unveiling Chertsey War Memorial
30th October 1921

There was one happy event after the war that cheered me up. My younger brother Laurence, who was in his forties and still a bachelor, had met a delightful lady Ellen, about ten years younger than him and they were clearly very much in love. They got married in January 1919 at St Paul's Church where we'd all gone as children. It was a lovely service and such a delight to see him settled and happy after all these years.

In the years after the war, I loved seeing all my little grandchildren. One of my fond memories is of Sydie with little Sonny all dressed up for the pageant on their float to raise money for the hospital at Windsor. They took a photograph outside one of the houses in Windsor Street and even made a postcard of it. So it was strange seeing pictures of the family for sale in the shops.

Grandchild Sonny (Sydney) during the Chertsey Pageant
Raising Money for Windsor Hospital
Taken outside Curfew House in Windsor Street 1924
Home of Dr. Pritchard

I carried on living at 27 Grove Road with some of the children though they were all grown up now. Over time all the family moved on having families of their own. It was a source of great comfort and pleasure to me to see them all established. How proud Syd would have been of every one of his children and grandchildren."

CHERTSEY WAR MEMORIAL

Chertsey War memorial was unveiled on 30th October 1921. The ceremony was attended by Lieutenant Colonel Clare and the Bishop of Guildford. The sculptor was Joseph Whitehead who was born in 1868, and worked from the age of about 20 in the family firm, J. Whitehead and Co. of London. Whitehead's standing figure of a soldier raising his helmet is apparently one of his best known pieces. It was cast at the foundry of A.B. Burton of Thames Ditton.

The memorial consists of a base surmounted by plinth and the bronze figure of a solider in battledress standing in Flanders mud. The inscriptions on the sides of the plinth read:

> ***'1914-1919 TO THE HONOURED MEMORY OF THE MEN OF CHERTSEY WHO FELL IN THE GREAT WAR ALSO IN GRATEFUL RECOGNITION OF ALL THOSE WHO FOUGHT IN THE WAR'***

The later addition after the Second World War reads:

> ***'ALSO OF THOSE 1939-1945 WHO GAVE THEIR LIVES IN THE SECOND WORLD WAR'***

The names of the fallen are inscribed on the faces of the plinth.

Whitehead used the same design for memorials in Worthing and Stafford. His model depicts a soldier holding a rifle in one hand, his other waving his helmet up in the air angled out from his body. He appears to be young but careworn with his tunic detailed with the combat dress of an infantry man with a variety of pockets, water flask and a backpack. He stands atop the detritus of war – clods of earth, a large shell, and a magazine of a machine gun with a ribbon of bullets lying discarded at his feet. He gives the impression of a man clearly affected by the war he has experienced but now triumphant that it has ended.

The Chertsey War Memorial is situated outside the parish church of St. Peter's, and is positioned prominently at the major road junction in the centre of the town where London Street, Guildford Street and Windsor Street meet. It was clearly meant as a focal point for the residents and to be seen by anyone driving through the town.

The unveiling was attended by a huge number of the local people and was extensively photographed and subsequently publicised by a number of postcards. It remains a focal point for the town to this day.

Chertsey War Memorial

WOMENS SUFFRAGE

At the start of the Great War, the right to vote was not as universal to over 18s as it is today. After the Third Reform Act in 1884, less than two thirds of male householders over the age of 21 had the vote. This left almost 40% of the over 18s who did not, and therefore, without a change in the law, millions of soldiers returning from the war would still not have been entitled to vote in the long overdue general election despite having fought for their country. No women were entitled to vote at this time. The issue of a female right to vote came to prominence during the latter half of the nineteenth century.

The Suffragettes and Suffragists had been pushing for, but denied, their right to be represented prior to the war, despite the increasing intensity of their campaign. This included direct action and even violent agitation encouraged by Emmeline Pankhurst and the Women's Social and Political Union.

There was some local action in and around Chertsey, taken by the suffragettes. Sir George and Lady White's mansion at Englefield Green was the subject of an arson attack and one of the suspects, Phyllis Brady, having evaded arrest for ten months, was eventually caught and bought to court in Chertsey.

SUFFRAGETTE ARSON CHARGE.

After evading the police for ten months, Phyllis Brady, a Suffragette, was charged at Chertsey to-day with setting fire to the residence of Lady White, widow of Sir George White, at Englefield Green, Egham, during the night of March 19, 1913.

Accused, a young woman, appeared in charge of prison wardresses.

James Kemble, a gardener, said that the house contained twenty rooms, which were practically all destroyed by the fire. The house was unoccupied at the time. Only the servants' hall was saved. Subsequently the remains of cans and bottles were discovered in a position which would have been underneath the stairs.

Early witnesses on the scene said the fire apparently started near the stairs.

Constable Alexander stated that he passed the house at 11.30 on March 19, and apparently nothing was amiss. An hour later two women passed him, cycling very fast from the direction of the house, and almost immediately he heard of the fire.

Two porters at Vauxhall Station spoke to two women carrying portmanteaus and possessing bicycles leaving for Staines by train on March 19; one of the porters, named White, said the accused closely resembled one of the women.

Westminster Gazette
Saturday 17th January 1914

In 1918 an Act of Parliament titled the Representation of the People Act, widened suffrage by abolishing practically all property qualifications for men, and enabled all men aged 21 and over to vote. It also enfranchised women over 30 who met certain minimum property qualifications. The enfranchisement of women was widely accepted as recognition of the contribution made by women during the War particularly in the defence industries. However, women were still not politically equal to men (who could vote from the age of 21).

More action by female suffragettes occurred during the 1920s with the aim of establishing equality in voting rights. Full electoral equality did not occur in Britain until a further Representation of the People Act in 1928.

The Representation of the People Act 1918 is sometimes known as the Fourth Reform Act. The Act extended the franchise in parliamentary elections, also known as the right to vote, to men aged 21 and over, whether or not they owned property; and to women aged 30 and over, who resided in the constituency, or occupied land or premises with a rateable value above £5, or whose husbands did.

As a result of the Act, the male electorate was extended by 5.2 million to 12.9 million. The female electorate was 8.5 million. The Act also created new electoral arrangements; including making residence in a specific constituency the basis of the right to vote; institutionalising the first-past-the-post method of election; and rejecting proportional representation.

Lizzy exercised her very first vote early that day in December 1918 and this did not pass unnoticed. A reporter from the press was there and this event was picked up by other provincial newspapers. The Oxfordshire Weekly News reported briefly on women voters in various towns including Chertsey, on that historic day when women were first able to cast their votes in a General Election.

booth.

One of the first voters in the Richmond division, where women outnumbered the men by four to one, was an old lady of 79. A girl of 12 wanted to vote for her mother, and was greatly disappointed when permission was refused.

At Kingston-on-Thames there was a steady stream of women voters all day, about 10 women to one man. Some of the women were so aged they leaned heavily on walking-sticks. A number of women were aided in voting by their husbands, but the majority came to the polling-booths alone.

At Chertsey two women opened the polling, where 19 persons on one estate found themselves not on the lists.

The oldest voter in Walthamstow was a woman of 91, who was an early arrival at the polling-booth.

Miss Emily Phipps, believing that many women in the poorer parts of Chelsea would bring their small children with them, had arranged to have women to take care of the babies while their mothers voted.

There was something reminiscent of Suffragette processions in the Sandwich women of Chelsea, who paraded the street with boards inscribed, "Vote for Phipps"; "Will Chelsea be the first to return a woman candidate?"

At Chiswick it was a "basket and baby election." The women voters brought big market baskets and carried babes in their arms or wheeled them up to the door in perambulators. At one time there were seven perambulators outside the Town Hall.

Extract from Oxfordshire Weekly News
Wednesday 18th December 1918

POSTSCRIPT

Little remains to be told of Lizzie's story other than to briefly tidy up some loose ends of what happened to Lizzie's large family after the Great War, including:

- Tom worked as a policeman after the war and then later became a Grill Chef in Lambeth, London. He and Violet had two sons, Eric and Stanley.
- Sydney continued to live in 10 Grove Road Chertsey and worked as head gardener at Monks Grove, a large house by St. Anne's Hill Chertsey, before losing his job in the great depression. He later became groundsman at the 'Rec' (Recreation Ground) nearby to Sir William Perkin's School. He and Doll had two children, Sydney and Ursula. Lizzie lived to see Syd play trombone in the town band and Ursie represent her county at swimming.
- Albert married Alice moving to Southgate, Middlesex, where he worked as a police constable and had a daughter, Sheila.
- Frederick married Millicent (Millie) Ward, moving to Esher where he worked as a police constable. They had three children, Elizabeth, Olive and Bernard.
- Edith and Reg with their daughter Myrtle, lived with Lizzie for some years and later moving to Staines Lane Chertsey. Reg worked as an Ironmonger's Fitter.
- Clara married Richard Ward, a gas fitter, and they lived at 41 Grove Road with their 4 children, Rhona, Daphne, Josephine and Ronald.
- Ruth married William Taylor, a bricklayer, and lived at 47 St Ann's Road, just round the corner from Grove Road and with their daughter Patricia.
- Alice had a son, Dennis and married George Smith.
- Lawrence moved to Maidstone in Kent where he also worked as a police constable. He was married twice with three children, John, Valerie and Michael.

After a long and eventful life with very challenging and turbulent times, Lizzie died in September 1933 aged 70, in her home town of Chertsey. Fondly and lovingly remembered by all her children and grandchildren, Lizzie would be completely unaware that she would become the subject of a biography nearly a century later authored by her great-grandson.

FAMILY TREE

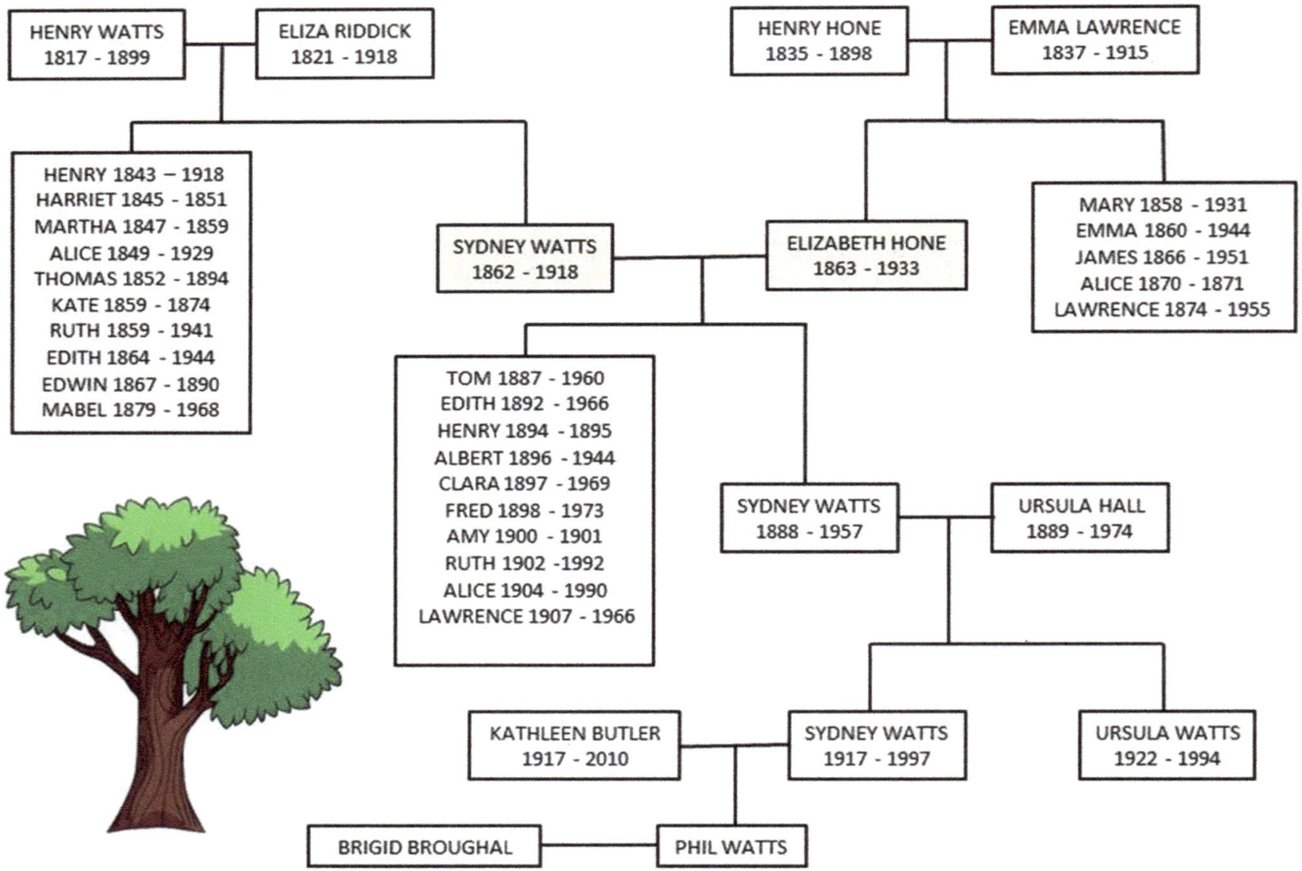
HENRY WATTS 1817 - 1899
ELIZA RIDDICK 1821 - 1918
HENRY HONE 1835 - 1898
EMMA LAWRENCE 1837 - 1915
HENRY 1843 – 1918
HARRIET 1845 - 1851
MARTHA 1847 - 1859
ALICE 1849 - 1929
THOMAS 1852 - 1894
KATE 1859 - 1874
RUTH 1859 - 1941
EDITH 1864 - 1944
EDWIN 1867 - 1890
MABEL 1879 - 1968
SYDNEY WATTS 1862 - 1918
ELIZABETH HONE 1863 - 1933
MARY 1858 - 1931
EMMA 1860 - 1944
JAMES 1866 - 1951
ALICE 1870 - 1871
LAWRENCE 1874 - 1955
TOM 1887 - 1960
EDITH 1892 - 1966
HENRY 1894 - 1895
ALBERT 1896 - 1944
CLARA 1897 - 1969
FRED 1898 - 1973
AMY 1900 - 1901
RUTH 1902 -1992
ALICE 1904 - 1990
LAWRENCE 1907 - 1966
SYDNEY WATTS 1888 - 1957
URSULA HALL 1889 - 1974
KATHLEEN BUTLER 1917 - 2010
SYDNEY WATTS 1917 - 1997
URSULA WATTS 1922 - 1994
BRIGID BROUGHAL
PHIL WATTS

ACKNOWLEDGEMENTS AND SOURCES

Family history, memorabilia, photographs and newspaper cuttings: These were gathered and stored by my father in a large box, which were then handed down to me. These items were gathering dust, for many years, until several years ago when I began to research my family tree. Fortunately, my father, Lizzie's grandson, had an amazing memory and he had always been a very methodical man. Therefore, unlike many collections of family photos, most are named, dated and described, and where necessary with an explanation of the relationship within the family.

Personal collection of old postcards: Over many years I have collected over 250 postcards of Chertsey, mostly from the period 1900 – 1930. The plan was (and still is) to establish a website with the old postcards of Chertsey alongside current photographs of the same scene showing the changes over a period of approximately 100 years. This particular project has never quite made it to the top of the 'to do' list. While my father was alive, I would send him my latest postcard acquisitions and he would reply with information about the card, the shops, the people, and the events of the time. Much of this information has proved invaluable in understanding the context of Lizzie's life in Chertsey. As examples, two postcards and his annotations are shown at the end of this section.

National Library of Scotland: Acknowledgement is gratefully given for the maps of Chertsey on pages 11 & 12 which are reproduced with the permission of the National Library of Scotland. Their excellent website can be found at: https://maps.nls.uk/index.html

Chertsey Museum: based at the Cedars, Windsor Street which is a wonderful source of local information and artefacts. Acknowledgement is gratefully given for their kind permission to reproduce the photographs on pages 32, 35, 36 & 37. Their excellent website may be found at: https://chertseymuseum.org/

Surrey History Centre: Woking, Surrey. An amazing collection of records of Surrey's past and present, documenting the story of the county and its people from the 12th century to the 21st century.

Thomas Coram Foundling Museum London: A stunning and very moving place to visit to learn about the work of Thomas Coram Hospital and the impact that it had on the children in the greatest need. It is located at: 40 Brunswick Square, Bloomsbury, London WC1N 1AZ Website: https://foundlingmuseum.org.uk/

The National Archives: Among many other areas of research, the source for the Army Records of the sons of Lizzie Watts. https://www.nationalarchives.gov.uk/

Ancestry: This provided an excellent start for my researching and assembling the details of my family tree. www.ancestry.co.uk

UK Census data: – accessed through Ancestry for the years 1841 - 1911

British Newspaper Archives: An incredible collection of digitised newspapers from the 1700s. The site has over 38m pages available. www.britishnewspaperarchive.co.uk

Wikipedia: An invaluable free resource on the web and a surprisingly helpful source for verifiable sources of information. The links from articles can lead to some surprising sources that might have been difficult to find otherwise. www.wikipedia.org

Google Maps: https://www.google.com/maps

U boats in World War 1: Provides detailed listings of all U-boats, their commanders and their activities. https://uboat.net/wwi/

Ships sunk in WW1: There are several sources for information in this area including: http://www.roll-of-honour.com/RoyalNavy/WarshipsLostWW1.html

https://www.nationalarchives.gov.uk/help-with-your-research/research-guides/ships-wrecked-sunk/

https://en.wikipedia.org/wiki/List_of_maritime_disasters_in_World_War_I

University of Leicester: Special Collections Online. Historical Directories of England & Wales and a collection of trade and local directories for England and Wales from the 1760s to the 1910s. Available at: http://specialcollections.le.ac.uk/digital/collection/p16445coll4

Glanfield, John. Bravest of the Brave: Book published in 2005 pp. 110–112 Sutton Publishing ISBN 0-7509-3695-9

Great War Fiction: https://greatwarfiction.wordpress.com/2016/02/26/shackletons-novels/

MacDonald, Lyn. The Roses of No Man's Land: Book published in 1993 Penguin Books P252, 259 ISBN 978-0-241-95240-5

The Wartime Memories Project - Tell Us Your Story:

https://www.wartimememoriesproject.com/greatwar/

Researching soldiers of the British Army in the Great War of 1914-1919:

https://www.longlongtrail.co.uk/

1914-1918-online. International Encyclopedia of the First World War:

https://encyclopedia.1914-1918-online.net/home/

Palmer Svetlana & Wallis Sarah A War in Words Book published in 2003 Simon & Schuster UK ISBN 0-7434-6906-2

Sample Chertsey Postcard and copy of my father's annotations & accompanying notes

1920 ST PETERS CHURCH AND
WINDSOR ST. CHERTSEY. OR 1921

POST W.W.I CARD PRIOR TO 1922. (NO WAR MEMORIAL)
FIRE ALARM (EDGE OF) IN EXTREME RIGHT OF RAILINGS.
THE VAN, OUTSIDE OF MADELEYS GROCERY SHOP, BELONGS
TO E.A. KIMBER, LOCAL SHIPPING AGENT, CARTER AND
COALMERCHANT, OFFICES NEXT TO CHERTSEY R/WAY
STATION YARD, THE DRIVER WAS LIKELY TO HAVE BEEN
RICHARD (DICK) LUIESLEY OF PYRCROFT RD.. I REMEMBER
THE PURE WHITE HORSE. NEXT DOOR TO MADELEYS WAS
BARNES (HERCULES CYCLE SHOP), "ELDRIDGES" THE SWAN
HOTEL & DENMARK HSE, (FAMILY HOME) & SURREY HERALD
OFFICE CAN BE CLEARLY SEEN IN L/H REAR.

Typical details and background context in my father's notes including noting that this photo was shot from Madeley's shop where my Great Grandfather worked for so many years.

THE UNVEILING OF CHERTSEY WAR MEMORIAL 20th OCT 1921

YOU WILL SEE THAT THE YEAR IS OFTEN GIVEN IN ERROR AS 1922. YOUR G/F IS STANDING IMMEDIATELY BELOW THE COMMA OF D.S.O. I REMEMBER THIS OCCASSION, DAD WENT ALONE AS MUM WAS HEAVY WITH URSIE (CONFIRMS YEAR). THE MEMORIAL WAS DRAPED WITH FLAGS WHICH FELL FOR THE OPENING. THE FIRST HYMN WAS "OH VALIANT HEART" THIS P.C. WAS TAKEN A LITTLE LATTER IN THE CEREMONY, FROM ONE OF MADELEY'S UPPER WINDOWS. COL. CLARE D.S.O. M.C LEFT CHERTSEY IN THE LATE 20s & ABBEY CHASE (HIS HOME) WAS TAKEN OVER BY TOM WALLS THE ACTOR, WHERE HE KEPT HIS DERBY WINNER "APRIL THE FIRST" AT STUD. THE W/M BECAME ONE OF MAIN POINTS FOR TOWN CRIER & DURING THE SLUMP OF 27/32. THE UNEMPLOYED GATHERED THERE HOPING TO BE CALLED TO RUN AN ERRAND (USUALLY FOR A WOODBINE CIG) THE NAME OF THE FALLEN IN W.W. II WERE ADDED TO THE NAME OF W.W.I IN 1947. SOME OF MY BOYHOOD PALS & SCH PUPILS —

RESTORATION OF PHOTOGRAPHS

Many of the illustrations I have used in this book are from family records dating back over 100 years, from postcards of a similar vintage, and from digitised newspaper records. In many instances there has been significant deterioration or damage sustained over the years. In order that these items could serve their purpose of supporting and illustrating my text, some restoration was necessary. I spent many hours working on this, staring at the computer monitor trying to judge whether an adjustment was actually an improvement or not. The program I used most was an open source photo editing software called FastStone. I found this more straightforward to use than Photoshop and other programs while still giving the necessary tools for restoration and enhancement. An example of before and after is shown on the next page. While it might be argued that the originals could have been used to show their true vintage and authenticity, I felt that it was equally important to be able to appreciate the visual content and detail wherever possible.

The results of these restorations are certainly not perfect! I fear that to achieve this would have meant many more hours spent sat at the computer. However I hope overall that they represent an improvement and enable the reader to appreciate them closer to their original condition, as pictorial evidence to support the narrative of Lizzie Watts and her times.

CPSIA information can be obtained
at www.ICGtesting.com
Printed in the USA
LVHW071615281021
701776LV00011BA/505

9 781913 460440